LANGUAGE AND INTELLIGENCE

LANGUAGE AND INTELLIGENCE

BY

JOHN HOLLOWAY

ARCHON BOOKS

1971

First Published 1951 by
Macmillan & Co. Ltd., London
Reprinted 1971 with permission
in an unaltered and unabridged
edition

THE SHOE STRING PRESS, INC.
Hamden, Connecticut 06514

Library of Congress Catalog Card Number: 70-131374
International Standard Book Number: 0-208-01115-3
Printed in the United States of America

PREFACE

I AM deeply indebted to Professor G. Ryle for invaluable guidance during the earlier stages of preparing this book, and for encouragement with it at all times; and to Dr. F. Waismann, to whose assistance, both by the printed word and in discussion, the last two chapters owe a great deal. Neither of these, though, can be held necessarily to share the opinions expressed, or accept their exact formulation.

I am also most grateful to Mr. J. L. Austin for several valuable suggestions about preparation and arrangement, and to Mr. J. L. Hevesi for permission to make use of an important point from so far unpublished work of his own, enabling me to clarify the argument of the earlier part of Chapter VII.

J. H.

CONTENTS

INTRODUCTION

UNTIL recently there was an established and integrated philosophical corpus, of problems if not of solutions to them, which covered the field of epistemology as well as of logic. It might be called " the classical position ". Though it left scope for major doctrinal differences, it was united in certain fundamentals ; and by many contemporary philosophers it has been decisively rejected.

The rejection has taken two forms : attacks upon the classical position, and independent progress towards another. The attacks were mainly directed against metaphysical thinking and the obscure language in which it was often expressed. Sometimes they examined with a new critical rigour the problems connected with universals. But the antagonism to metaphysics resulted from the positive side of the new outlook ; and this, moreover, has given every individual philosophical problem a new appearance, and transformed the discussion of it.

There is no closed and settled group of principles, which anyone would accept if he were sympathetic to this new approach ; but one can usually trace, among its followers, a certain community of interest, of method, and of solution. In the main, the new philosophical outlook has developed because the verbal language, in which the problems of philosophy are both expressed and resolved, has been thought of in a new way. This has been made possible first by developing formal logic and applying its techniques to ordinary language, and then by the realization that language and logic could not be identified. Thus the two were brought closer together, and then were moved apart. Of these two processes, the former claimed to emancipate symbols from an alleged dependence on thought as its mere expression; and the latter promoted them to a status of their own.

The new conception of language has given rise to certain important principles, and these have been applied to many particular philosophical problems. Among these principles are, that *a priori* propositions are in some sense verbal; that empirical propositions are significant because and as far as they can be verified; that words for empirical concepts are essentially vague in meaning; and that philosophical discussions often, or always, consist in recommending contrary verbal usages. There has been no appeal to these principles, as to established premises from which inferences might simply be drawn without comment. They have tended rather to guide every discussion in a certain direction.

But even if given no great prominence, they are quite incompatible with the classical position; and to its defenders they appear the more unplausible, because usually presented only as dogmas. They appear as dogmas, because the new philosophical outlook, as a whole, is less comprehensive than its forerunner. The classical position did not lack a theory about language, though it was seldom conspicuous and was presented, if at all, in a jargon which today is unpopular. But this theory would not have been brought forward as an independent dogma; it derived from a more general theory about thinking itself.

It is possible that the new outlook, or something not unlike it, could have developed from progress in psychology; and had this occurred, epistemology and the study of language would doubtless not have grown apart as they have. But the stimulus has been from formal logic; and this divorce between the two is the result. Perhaps it is not to be regretted. Through the amassing of new formal techniques, developments have been rigorous in style, and so more authoritative. Besides this, the philosophers of the newer school have tended to be competent mathematicians; and in the past mathematics has always presented the crucial difficulty for an empiricist. But in some respects the consequences have been unfortunate. Philosophers of the classical position have sometimes overlooked the restricted nature of the claim made for certain new formal devices, as happened with Russell's symbol for material implication. At other times they have argued that their opponents have been preoccupied with purely external aspects of language, and have overlooked problems in epistemology which raise prior questions for any proper theory of logic.

This important criticism gains strength by coinciding with a plain mistake not uncommon, at least at one time, among philosophers of the newer school. Through what was probably a logical confusion connected with the problem of our knowledge of other minds, they have frequently thought themselves committed to some version of philosophical behaviourism. In view of this extravagance, one could not have been surprised if, though perhaps plausible within the linguistic sphere, their outlook was thought to be inadequate for the whole scope of philosophy.

It is thus objected against the new philosophical outlook that it neglects the epistemological factors involved in the use of symbols; and more particularly, that it offers no account of the distinction between their automatic and unthinking use, and the genuine movement of thought. If this objection could not be met, the new theory would be gravely deficient; and how it may be overcome is the central problem of this work.

But the classical position itself is less comprehensive than is claimed; on examination, its scope is seen to be significantly restricted. In the first place, there is no simple contrast between the unthinking or stupid use of symbols, and their genuine or intelligent use. Verbal intelligence can be manifested to a great or small degree; it is more present, or less. The classical account of genuine thought is that it results from an awareness of universals or concepts, while no such awareness accompanies stupid quasi-thought or mere talking. This dichotomy does not readily lend itself to the explanation of a smoothly gradu-ated scale of displayed intelligence; and indeed no attempt has been made to give such an explanation, though it would be rash and perhaps false to say that it could not have been given.

There are more serious objections, however, to the older theory of intelligent thought. It suffered from one incompleteness at least as striking as that with which its adherents tax their opponents. Whether or not it was an adequate account of intelligent thinking, it said little or nothing of how intelligence was manifested in other activities. But to examine thought thus in the void will not do; partly because an arbitrary restriction of interest is alien to the spirit of philosophical enquiry, chiefly because the empirical evidence suggests that the restriction led to error. The theory was obliged to make other in-telligent activities parasitic upon intelligent thought; and it is possible to do so only in defiance of the facts.

The problems, how genuine is to be distinguished from quasi-thinking, and how symbols have meaning, are connected more intimately than has been realized. The latter problem, taken as the starting-point of this work, necessarily introduces the former; and if they are examined together, it becomes clear that neither can be finally solved except in a context wide enough to include the general range of human behaviour. Of this range, using symbols is but one part; and it cannot be assumed that this part is unique and self-sufficient.

In order to discuss the general features of behaviour,

intelligent and otherwise, it is necessary to have one expression for whatever prompts or induces an agent to act in a certain way, and another for the behaviour which constitutes his act. With some hesitation, I have used the words " stimulus " and " response ". They will probably be accepted as valid for the most primitive levels of behaviour; whether and how they are applicable to the higher levels is a guiding question. The danger of any philosophical terminology lies in its power to blind us to empirical facts which do not fit our theory, and to induce acceptance of convenient figments of the imagination as facts in their place. I hope that vigilance against this danger has sufficed to avert it.

No attempt is made to give a definition of intelligence, or a formula which would establish its presence or absence in every case. Such attempts are chimerical. But there are varieties of behaviour, even among animals, which make the word " intelligence " necessary. Then one can discuss how intelligent and routine performances are akin, and how they differ; and examine what may be said of how an intelligent performance originates, in order to refute certain parts of the classical account. Certain empirical facts are given consideration; but they are not detailed and technical, or such as concern experimental psychologists. They are of that very general kind for which philosophers perhaps display an excessive interest. No criticism, even implicit, is made of the empirical work of psychologists, save where they have incorporated into it the classical position of philosophy. But such a process of incorporation is less common than it was.

Certain criticisms are also made of the newer school of philosophy; for there is no doubt that its preoccupation with the formal aspects of language has been regrettable. A quite excessive emphasis was thereby thrown on the descriptive function of symbols; and sentential expressions were abstracted from the particular conditions of their

utterance, which confused the problem of symbolic meaning and made it impossible to describe the effect of certain
verbal expressions. Most important, the general features
of the verbal language have been presented, often enough,
as an unexplained surprise; whereas one should have
expected them, and no others. An attempt is made here
to remedy these deficiencies, by utilizing the distinction
between speech and language, which Saussure and Gardiner
long ago made familiar, if not to philosophers, at least to
all others whom it concerned.

From this perspective, the general problem presents a
new appearance. That theory of language which is integral
to the contemporary philosophical outlook is seen largely
to derive from the status of the verbal or symbol-using
activity, merely as one form of human behaviour. When
behaviour in general has been discussed, the argument
examines the use of language in actual speech, first at a
simple and then at more advanced levels. This reveals
how intimately speech and other forms of behaviour are
related in any activity which communicates a meaning.
It shows too how the significance of certain verbal elements
can be understood only in a context wider than that of
speech. The final step is to examine the verbal language
in isolation; it is by far the most developed means of
communication, and it deserves special attention. Even
its most sophisticated varieties are seen to reflect the
features of behaviour in general, and of symbol-using
behaviour in particular.

The underlying purpose of this work is therefore to
show that those principles — empiricist, positivist, or
linguistic in trend — which constitute together what
might be termed the " contemporary position ", need not
be assessed in isolation. So far from being independent
of our general understanding of human behaviour, or an
isolated exception to it, they are exactly the principles
which it would lead us to expect. Indeed, the theory of

universals, underlying everywhere the answers given in
the classical position, is what stands in isolation ; for it is
an account invented for one fragment of human activity
by thinkers oblivious of the rest of it. The foundation
of the older philosophy is artificial, and peculiar, and in
pressing need of demonstration at every point ; that of the
newer, such that if anything may ever be taken for granted,
this might be ; and one notices, when a discussion between
non-philosophers hovers for a moment on the brink of
philosophy, that it not infrequently is.

CHAPTER I

IDEAS AND IMAGES

W E have claimed that some theory of how symbols have meaning, how they can occur not automatically but in genuine thought, must form the general substructure of any philosophical position. But it would be unreasonable to advance a theory independently, unless an examination of the established theories showed them to be inadequate. This first chapter, therefore, will dissect the theory that symbols have meaning through their association with mental imagery, and the second, that they have it through association with universals or concepts. These are the two theories most likely to find support at present. The second is the real basis of the " classical position " ; but the first also merits examination, since this focusses attention on some of the obvious pitfalls, and the obvious truths, which mark out the whole problem.

The theory that meaning is a derivation from imagery is also important because in one form or another it was adopted by Locke, Berkeley, and Hume ; and these philosophers have so much influenced modern philosophy, that contemporary writers have very often envisaged the problem in their terms, whatever answer they might give to it. We shall begin therefore with their discussions, in order to see the " problem of meaning " in the proportions given it by that initial formulation.

Locke expressed the problem in the following way : " All things that exist being particulars, it may perhaps be thought reasonable that words, which ought to be conformed to things, should be so too; I mean in their signification: but yet we find the quite contrary. The far greatest part of words that make all languages are general." [1] Then he proceeds to ask what endows them with generality. But although he plainly sees the problem, he offers no one consistent solution to it. He makes several incompatible suggestions, but no attempt to reconcile them. Probably he did not realize how his remarks contradicted each other.

Berkeley [2] did not disentangle the varied and incompatible suggestions which Locke put forward. His criticisms are relevant to some, and irrelevant to others. There are in fact two suggestions of Locke's to which they are relevant; and these have an important common characteristic, for they both rest upon the assumption that terms are general in meaning because they *name* a certain type of entity, just as " Peter " might name another type of entity, a particular dog. As Berkeley interprets Locke's theory, the entities which provide meanings for general terms are images. There are two views because these images may be thought of in two different ways. The first, rendered plausible by considering general terms like " whiteness ", is that the images are truncated or schematic images, left behind after a process of eliminating fortuitous characteristics from many particular images; the " abstract general ideas " preserve only the essential characteristics. The second, rendered plausible by considering general terms like " triangle ", suggests that general ideas are not schematic but comprehensive, and include within themselves all the possible varieties of the sort which they represent.

Berkeley denies this theory of comprehensive images by arguing that no image can combine two or more variations of the same quality. He thinks this so clearly true

---

[1] *Essay concerning Human Understanding*, III, iii, 1.
[2] *The Principles of Human Knowledge*, Introduction, etc.

that it needs little or no emphasis. He devotes more time
to the theory of schematic or skeleton-images presenting
essences; in his opinion, neither abstraction nor any other
mental process can conceivably produce images of this kind.
Images must be specific and complete; it is impossible to
have, for instance, a visual image of the colour of an apple,
unless combined with the shape, either of the apple or of
some other thing. If I imagine a triangle, its three sides
must be of definite sizes in relation to each other, and
so must its angles; if I imagine a second triangle, that
must be clearly bigger or smaller in area than the first, or
equal to it. It means nothing to speak of triangles which
have no specific characteristics, but all and none of the
whole imaginable variety of colour, figure, and the rest.
Neither comprehensive nor schematic images can exist;
and if they cannot exist, they cannot explain how general
terms have generality of meaning.

These arguments convinced Berkeley that no image
could function as an abstract general idea in the way that
(he believed) Locke had supposed. But (except for
notions, which he thought were relevant only to certain
very special words, and which were in fact quite incompatible with the rest of his theory) Berkeley held that
images were nevertheless the sole furniture of the mind.
Thus he could solve the problem which he had accepted
only by rejecting Locke's basic assumption. He was
obliged to deny that if a word has generality of meaning,
it must name some entity which is essentially general.

Generality must not be sought, he claims, in the
" absolute *positive* nature " of an idea of a unique kind,
to which the term stands in a simple relation. It must be
sought in the complex relation which holds between one
particular and many others.[1] An idea becomes general
by being made to " represent " or " stand for " other ideas
of the same sort. Nor does a word possess a general

[1] Introduction to *The Principles of Human Knowledge*, para. 15.

meaning because it stands for and names a general idea;
but because it is made the sign of " several particular ideas,
any one of which it indifferently suggests to the mind ".[1]
He notes elsewhere that the representative idea " doth
equally stand for and represent " all possible examples of
the class of which it is a member.

Clearly, he is here thinking of images; his discussion
of the " idea I have in view " [2] in following demonstrations
of geometry, puts this beyond doubt. The representative
function need not be carried out every time by one and
the same image. Our representative image of " cat ", the
plenipotentiary of all the images we could summon up,
might sometimes be one sort of a cat, and sometimes
another. Any image may occupy the privileged position
of a representative idea, an idea that has acquired a general
meaning; it is a representative idea only because it can call
up or suggest its fellows.

There are now two main problems. One is whether
Berkeley's criticisms of the theories he attributes to Locke
are valid; and the other, whether his own theory is valid.

Berkeley clearly used the word " idea " to mean what
" image " means today. But if so, his conclusion that all
ideas must be fully determinate is false. Testimony
suggests that, for most people, visual images are so blurred
or faint or unsteady that their precise colour and shape
could not be put into words. Memory and imagination
images are woolly or schematic in a characteristic way;
they lack the sharp outline, the clear colours, and the
detail which distinguish some impressions. The mental
image which is " as clear as life " is rare and surprising.
Berkeley would have been prepared, in part, to admit these
points. But his theoretical assumptions seem to have
persuaded him that images must nevertheless be determinate in every detail; and he failed to notice how the

[1] Introduction to *The Principles of Human Knowledge*, para. 11.
[2] *Ibid.* para. 16.

facts of psychology showed that these general assumptions were misleading him.

There is no need to suppose, however, that if images are in some sense indeterminate, they must be of a puzzling status, and quite different from the impressions of sense. This absence of sharpness and clarity, distinguishing them from some impressions, is what makes them similar to others; and the latter class of impressions is very much larger than the former. Of the impressions of sight, only those at the centre or focal region of the visual field are sharp and clear; all the others are more or less schematic, fuzzy, and undetermined, and are very similar to visual imagery. Moreover, not sight alone, but every sense gives sensations which are vague and indefinite. Nothing is more likely than that mental imagery should be indefinite too.

Berkeley's description of mental imagery is therefore erroneous. But this does not affect the substance of his argument. His criticisms of what he believes to be Locke's theories remain valid. Berkeley tried to prove more than he needed. Images may sometimes be indeterminate and fuzzy; but this gives no support to the theories he attacked, for they require more. The theory of skeleton-ideas requires that the mental image should sharply exclude all qualities which are not essential to the meaning of the word naming the idea. The theory of comprehensive ideas requires that an image should definitely combine all the possible varieties and modifications of the sort. To accept less than this would be to accept an undetermined meaning for the word. Neither of these theories receives the least support from the vagueness and woolliness of mental imagery.

Now for Berkeley's positive view. It is stated clearly enough in *The Principles of Human Knowledge*, but there is something curiously terse about the statement. He accuses Locke of the unconscious assumption that words have general meaning because they name general entities, and of supposing that his problem was solved by the production of the entity in question — necessarily, Berkeley argues, a monster. But he too made unconscious assumptions. Here his assumption seems to be that a word would have a general meaning if it *represented*; and that the problem is solved by showing that, to something or other, it stands in a relation of representing. But he never analyses this relation of " equally representing " or " indifferently standing for ", though his whole theory depends upon it.

In one place he suggests that a word is " made " the sign of several particular ideas, and that in consequence of being appointed to this position it is able to " suggest " them to the mind.[1] But he seems never to have considered whether a term suggests because it represents, or is able to represent because already it suggests.

Hume's discussion [2] of how words have general meanings follows Berkeley closely; but in this respect he adds considerably to the theory. He decides, first that the word and the particular ideas are associated by constant conjunction in fact, and second, that term and ideas are consequently related in the mind by a settled habit. Because of this habit, the word recalls to the imagination one or more of the particular ideas, and conversely the particular ideas recall the word.

Hume believes that although he cannot explain why habits of this kind can be formed at all, he can say something about their general character. A single habit is developed towards objects which resemble each other; and it will be extended to fresh objects, provided that they resemble the objects through experience of which it was first acquired. Moreover, there is nothing mysterious in a habit whereby words suggest ideas, and ideas words, for there are several other mental processes which depend on

---

[1] Introduction to *The Principles of Human Knowledge*, para. 11.
[2] *Treatise of Human Nature*, Book I, 1, 7.

suggestion through habitual association. Counting is an instance. We can count far beyond the numbers for which we can have illustrative images, because of a settled habit of using number-words whereby each expression suggests to our mind that which follows in the series. Reciting by heart is another instance; here also one word suggests those which follow, by virtue of a habit acquired from constant association.

It was perspicacious of Hume to recognize that the relation of representing must be analysed if his theory was to be complete, and he showed ingenuity in basing it upon an acquired habit of association and suggesting parallels to it. But he does not reach the crux of this problem. What he is unable to account for satisfactorily, is the critical nature of recollecting a series of particular ideas or images. He cannot explain the discrimination and selection with which we treat the series. He notices, it is true, that if a false generalization is made through failure to check words with the ideas they represent, then the crucial idea will present itself spontaneously and draw attention to the error. But more complicated processes also occur. An idea, for example, which might clinch or disprove some generalization may be rejected as not a genuine instance of the class. One might have formed the opinion that all swans are large birds. This opinion would not be modified if the image of a small porcelain swan came into mind. The image would be rejected as irrelevant, as not being an image of a real swan. But it satisfies Hume's conditions; it has occurred in a series of " ideas " prompted by a habit, and it resembles the other members.

According to this theory, the meaning of a word is determined exclusively by the series of ideas which hearing and seeing the word brings to mind. But there is no authoritative series; there is not even any one series which occurs in every case. Sometimes the habit or custom may evoke one series of ideas, and at other times a quite different series. There might not be a single idea common to both. But if the meaning of a term is determined exclusively by the succession of ideas which it evokes, then there can be no ground for accepting one manifestation of the habit as authentic, and rejecting another as not. The meaning of the word, and in consequence the truth or falsehood of statements in which it occurs, may vary from hour to hour. If a momentary breakdown in the habitual association prevents the crucial idea from coming to mind, the false generalization will be true.

Hume cannot explain how, although we may frequently call up, or let come into mind, a succession of images which guide us in the use of a word, yet this succession is critically considered; its constituents are accepted or rejected. This process reveals a reference to some pre-existing standard. For Hume this discrimination is inexplicable. The present manifestation of the habit in the succession of images simply constitutes the standard of meaning. It would be impossible for him to say, even, that we could recognize a particular series as defective, by remembering some authoritative past series. This recollection will simply be a new series which differs from its predecessor.

Sometimes Hume admits unconsciously that the series of resembling particulars is not accepted automatically, but may be critically tested. " Individuals ", he says, " are collected together and placed under a general term with a view to that resemblance which they bear to each other " ; or " when we have found a resemblance among certain objects, that often occur to us, we apply the same name to all of them ". Human beings might form habitual associations between similar experiences, much as flowers tend to grow towards the sunshine, or limpets to cling to the rocks. But to *find* a resemblance suggests more than this. It suggests that we notice, for example, that several objects all resemble each other in a certain way; and that we then decide to give a certain name to that common quality, by virtue of having which they do so resemble each other. The habit of association which accounts for meaning cannot be based on any resemblance of no matter what random kind, but only on a resemblance in a certain specific respect. But giving attention to this resemblance, and disregarding other respects in which the particulars may differ, Hume cannot explain.

The passage in which Hume discusses " distinctions of reason " makes the incompleteness of his theory disastrously clear. He shows a difference in meaning between " shape " and " colour " only by abandoning his main position. It is well known that however many particular ideas either word may bring by custom into the mind, every instance of the one is necessarily an instance of the other too. He claims that when considering the particular ideas we " view them in different aspects, according to the resemblances of which they are susceptible ". But " resemblance in colour " and " resemblance in shape " are, on his principles, simply not intelligible as different " aspects ", unless the two different words can evoke different series of ideas; and the whole difficulty arises because this is impossible. If we are to be able to ask, of a particular series of ideas, " Are the members of this series associated by resemblance in colour, or by resemblance in shape ? ", then the expressions in this question must be intelligible, independent of any connexion they may have with the series in question. But if so, they do not have meaning in the way that Hume supposed.

In discussing colour and shape, Hume admittedly gives a solution to the difficulty they raise which reveals the limitations of his own theory, and slips into a terminology which is inconsistent with it. But it should be said in fairness to him that he could have avoided this lapse. On the one hand, he could have argued plausibly though not perhaps conclusively that a visible point of light was coloured, but did not have a shape at all. If this were accepted, then the colour-series could contain members which did not appear in the shape-series. On the other hand, he could certainly have shown that there were ideas which could occur in the shape-series and not in the colour-series, and was only prevented from doing so by an unconscious assumption that mental images were necessarily of the visual kind. But this is untrue; images may be, for example, tactile; we have such images when we remember the feel of velvet or of ball-bearings, or remember what it is like to do up a button. Hume, if he had thought of it, could have pointed to these as ideas peculiar to the shape-series, and thus have provided himself with an indisputable difference. But in one way, perhaps, it is fortunate that this did not occur to him; for instead he chose a way out of his difficulty which emphasizes the general inadequacy of his solution.

If these suggestions are thought adequate to solve the special problem about shape and colour, then there are two techniques which might be employed to preserve the general outline of Hume's theory, while allowing for the element of discrimination which he ignored. In the first place, it might be said that the members of a series of ideas giving the meaning of a word resemble each other, and that in addition there is a resemblance between these resemblances. If resemblance is accepted as fundamental, it might be exploited in this way to show how we can critically assess the ideas which are suggested spontaneously. It might be argued, for example, that the idea of a porcelain swan is rejected because, although it resembles ideas of other swans, this resemblance is unlike the other resemblances, those between ideas of " genuine " swans. But this solution is quite specious. One can mean nothing at all by the expression " resembling resemblances ", unless it is defined by saying, for example, that resemblances resemble when they are of the same kind ; and once again, one is obliged to confess that the kind of resemblance in question can be intelligible, in advance of the idea-series which illustrates it. One is obliged to admit this, because one has admitted that understanding what is meant by that particular kind of resemblance, is what equips us to build up any series illustrating it, in a critical and discriminating way. It is impossible to say whether, of three resembling objects, the resemblance between the first and the second resembles that between the second and third, until the respect of resemblance, which is the criterion of resembling resemblance or its absence, has been specified. For example, in the case of three window-bars, the first and second vertical, and the third horizontal, all three resemble each other. But one cannot say outright whether the resemblance between first and second resembles that between second and third. One must be told what sort of resemblance is in question. If one uses this confusing terminology at all, one must say that the resemblances in respect of colour or linear visual quality resemble, but those in respect of degree of angular divergence, or of being vertical or horizontal, do not resemble. The whole terminology, however, was introduced only so that by its aid we could construct idea-series which could give meaning to " vertical " and " horizontal ", themselves.

The other technique for preserving the general outlines of Hume's theory is to analyse " resemblance in a certain respect ", so that it can be defined by reference to relations between particular ideas, some of which are acknowledged or " standard " members of the series of ideas in question. " When we see that two sense-impressions ' resemble each other in respect of being red ', we can say that they each resemble each other exactly as they resemble a third sense impression which we adopt as the standard example of 'red'." [1]

[1] S. Hampshire, " Ideas, Propositions, and Signs ", *Proceedings of the Aristotelian Society*, 1939–40, p. 15.

We might, indeed, take several standard objects as *ex-officio* members of the idea-series; and we could then establish, as our criterion of whether some subsequent idea was an authentic member or not, that it must resemble the standard members as closely as, or in the way that, they resemble each other. " If we are asked of a particular idea which is used as a sign, ' What does this mean ? ' we point to a group of particular ideas — ' it stands for this and for this, and for this, and for anything which resembles these as they resemble each other '." [1] It was shown in the preceding paragraph that reference to the sort of resemblance is of no avail in evading the difficulty; to refer to a resemblance as close as that between the standard objects is equally fruitless. This looks like succeeding, only if attention is restricted to quite abnormally simple cases. It seems plausible enough, for example, to take images of a pillar-box, a sheet of blotting-paper, and an apple, as standard instances of " red ", and assert that anything which resembles them as required is also red. But applied to more complex cases, every vestige of plausibility disappears. For if the standard ideas are to be typical (as normally they are supposed to be), it is plain that a very abnormal instance of the idea they typify resembles them far less closely than they resemble each other. On the other hand, it would be preposterous to take, as the standard ideas, those extreme and remarkable particulars which are just to be included within the meaning of the term : to take, say, a vessel propelled by windmill-sails, a Melanesian war-canoe, and a monitor, as standard examples of " ship ". It would be preposterous in a literal sense, because in fact they would be included in the idea-series for " ship ", after some hesitation, because we were already equipped in some way to decide its dimensions and boundaries.

The conclusions so far established are, in the first

[1] *Loc. cit.*

place, that the meaning of a word cannot be identified with the succession of ideas which the word evokes; this is impossible because the succession is itself critically checked and tested in a way which shows that it does not constitute the meaning, but depends on knowledge of it. Second, the meaning of the word cannot be identified with an " authentic " series, defined as one in which the resemblances resemble, because resemblances are seen to resemble only when they are seen all to be of a certain kind, and knowing this kind entails knowing the meaning of the word, prior to constructing the series which is alleged to endow it with meaning. Third, an " authentic " idea-series cannot be defined by reference to standard members and resemblances of equal closeness, because this would necessarily involve one or other of two impossible conditions : either we must say that resemblances are equally close when in fact they are not, or we must take as the standard members, from which the series is constructed, anomalous border-line cases which can only be included in the series when it has in the main been constructed already.

In each case the contradiction lies in identifying the meaning of the word with the idea-series, and arises because the construction of the series is a critical process ; and presupposes always that the meaning of the word in question is known already. Though there may be a close connexion between series and meaning, the idea-series can never be what is known when the meaning is known ; the idea-series cannot *be* the meaning. If this is so, Hume's analysis of the relation of representing or " standing for " must be rejected. So too must the attempts to refine his theory, by substituting, for his opinion that " representing " was the relation between word, and idea-series evoked by custom, the opinion that it was the relation between word, and idea-series not merely evoked but also critically checked and authenticated.

It is strange to discover that both Hume and Berkeley had noticed something which betrays the mistake in their analysis. Both of them had noticed how using and understanding words is really independent of those series of ideas which were supposed to give them significance. Berkeley seems to have confused two separate points in his discussion : sometimes he has in mind that words do not stand for ideas because they can be intelligible even if unaccompanied by ideas, and sometimes, that they do not stand for ideas when they are used emotively to express or evoke feelings. Only the former is relevant here ; and of it he says, " it is not necessary (even in the strictest reasonings) significant names which stand for ideas should, every time they are used, excite in the understanding the ideas they are made to stand for . . . general names are often used in the propriety of language without the speakers designing them for marks of ideas in his own, which he would have them raise in the mind of the hearer ".[1] Hume says, "We do not annex distinct and complete ideas to every term we make use of, and . . . in talking of *government*, *church*, *negotiation*, *conquest*, we seldom spread out in our minds all the simple ideas of which these complex ones are composed. It is however observable that, notwithstanding this imperfection, we may avoid talking nonsense on these subjects, and may perceive any repugnance among the ideas as well as if we had a full comprehension of them." [2] If we dismiss the possibility that this is simply a sly but irrelevant joke, it is fair to say that Hume, by using the expressions " imperfection " and " as if we had a full comprehension ", was here not alive to the significance of his observation.

If using and understanding words is possible in the absence of their corresponding idea-series, then the idea-series cannot be what the words mean. For in this case

[1] Introduction to *The Principles of Human Knowledge*, paras. 19, 20.
[2] *Loc. cit.*

we should, when we used or understood a word, know something and at the same time not know it. This apparent *impasse* should have drawn the attention of Berkeley and Hume to the problem; and had they attempted its solution by referring to a dispositional sense of " knowing ", they would have encountered the difficulties discussed above. It must be confessed that neither reached the crucial difficulties. Hume was too radical, perhaps, in his unqualified reliance upon habit, and not radical enough in accepting from Locke a diction which he did not completely free from ambiguity.

The value of the work done in this field by Berkeley and Hume should not be underestimated. Together they made several suggestions which were novel and important. They challenged Locke's assumption that the " signification " of a word was some single entity which the word named; they noticed that words could be intelligible by themselves; they avoided nebulous or shadowy mental entities, and referred only to imagery, with which most people are well acquainted; and finally, Hume at least emphasized the connexion between using verbal language and acquiring verbal habits. These principles are perennially fertile.

CHAPTER II

UNIVERSALS AND CONCEPTS

OF the whole array of problems or alleged problems about universals, this chapter will discuss only one: whether or not they, or concepts their partners, explain how words have meaning. This is of importance, it will be remembered, because to know the real difference between words used with meaning and words used with none, is to know the distinction between their intelligent and their mechanical use; and it is argued that this distinction cannot possibly be explained, unless either the concept or the universal is introduced.

Two theories of the nature of universals will be considered, the conceptualist belief that they are mental entities, and the *in re* form of realism which maintains that they inhere in objects and are so apprehended by the mind. The conceptualist theory was the first to be utilized in criticizing the speculations of Berkeley and Hume which were discussed in the last chapter. It was expressed by Reid [1] in these words: " as general words are so necessary in language, it is natural to conclude that there must be general conceptions, of which they are the signs ". The general conception is thus what the general word signifies, and therefore its meaning. Reid is clear that it is not an image. " I think we may be certain that universals are not conceived by means of images of them in our minds, because there can be no image of a universal." Berkeley and Hume, in his opinion, should have rejected,

---

[1] *Intellectual Powers of Man* (Essay V, Chapter 6).

not Locke's hypothesis that a process of abstraction could produce mental entities of a general kind, but his hypothesis that these entities were images. The general conception is a mental content which is different in kind from any image; and words have meaning because they are the signs of these mental contents. They are not simply found in particular material objects: " the conception of whiteness implies no existence ". They are a set of mental touchstones, part of the mind's equipment for recognizing the particular qualities which it perceives and for articulating this recognition in verbal form.[1]

The other theory to be discussed is the *in re* form of Realism; according to which, thinking is made possible by apprehending entities that are not mental contents, but exist externally in particular objects. Thus Cook-Wilson says, ". . . we cannot apprehend the definite quality of anything (say redness) without apprehending . . . a universal. This would be quite impossible if we had apprehended something merely particular and entirely confined to the particular instance." [2] This theory offers an account of how using language can be genuine thought, by asserting that each general word is the name of a certain entity. Uttering the word to describe an object is really thinking when it is based upon apprehending the universal which resides in that object, and when the word uttered is its name. Should the universal not be apprehended, then uttering even the right name is only a reflex noise.

Let us examine Cook-Wilson's form of the theory more closely. It asserts that when we say " that is red " on seeing a bus or a penny stamp, our utterance is genuine thought if and only if based on awareness of the universal " redness " present in the object. If we assert that the bus and the stamp are both red, it should be from recog-

---

[1] Compare B. Russell, *Knowledge by Acquaintance and Knowledge by Description*, published in *Mysticism and Logic* (1918), p. 209.
[2] *Statement and Inference*, i, p. 337.

C

nizing that a certain universal is common to them.

Perhaps this is an adequate explanation of how particular positive assertions of the form " that is red " can embody genuine thought; but one would expect the theory to account, if for any, then for all forms of statement about particular and present objects. Yet it does not seem to apply to sentences which compare one object with another in respect of a certain quality. According to the theory, saying " they are both red " of two apples must be based on an awareness that both instantiate the single universal redness. But suppose that one takes the comparison further and adds, " this apple is redder than that ". If this utterance is not to be a mere noise, it must be based on awareness of some universal. But the universal apprehended cannot now be redness, because both apples are red. Nor can it be some quality such as " being redder "; for the second apple " is redder " not in general, but only in relation to the first, and this is a particular fact about it. One is tempted to say that in one (or indeed in both) the universal redness is present in a more or less complete form. But this is self-contradictory; everything about the universal which distinguishes its instantiation in one case from its instantiation in another must itself be particular. If the universal is not always one and the same, then though it may be able to invest comparative sentences with a genuine quality, it becomes incapable of doing so for positive sentences; and this was its original function.

It is doubtful if this difficulty is avoided by saying that, for a comparative sentence, the relevant universal is a " relational quality ", *redder than* . . .; for this universal is clearly not instantiated by either apple, and its instantiation by the relation between them (whatever that might mean) would be enough to equip us to say, " one apple is redder than the other ", but not which. Moreover, every variation in the degree to which the one apple was redder than another, would involve a new universal apprehended in a different relation of " redder than ", while sentences of the form " *a* is redder than *b*, and *b* is redder than *c* " involve the original difficulty in a new form; for unless the degree of additional redness is identical in each case, then the same expression has been used, upon the basis of apprehending two different universals, two " redder thans " of differing degree; and since this is at variance with the original condition for being " genuine thought ", the expression is necessarily a reflex cry. At every turn we find ourselves prompted to erase the whole problem by saying that what is " apprehended " is simply " that this is redder than that ". But it is precisely this expression which is inadequate, because it refers to a particular state of affairs. The difficulty, it seems, is to translate the expression into terms of those universals which make it intelligible.

These difficulties are not confined to awareness of universals named by adjectives. They present themselves with equal force if we attempt to explain how such expressions as " nearly a tumble ", " scarcely a promise ", " easily a foul " can be more than automatisms. Clearly the awareness of universals adequate for the explanation cannot simply be, for example, an awareness of the universal " tumble " itself; for what requires explanation is that the event in question was not simply a tumble, but " nearly a tumble ". Nor can it be said that two universals are apprehended, " tumble " and " nearness ", because there was no tumble. Perhaps the universal apprehended is, once again, a relational property; this time between the particular event and the universal " tumble ". It is, however, difficult to analyse this property. It cannot be present by virtue of some universal other than " tumble ", instantiated by the particular event, for we are unaware of any such other universal; and it cannot be present because the particular event does instantiate " tumble ", for this would give us a relation of identity, and that the particular event is not identical with a tumble is just what we are trying to say. The relational property must be one which holds between the particular event itself and the universal " tumble ". But it is not the relation either of instantiation or of *not*-instantiation, and how can there be any others ? The same difficulty arises in the opposite direction with such expressions as " a thorough mess ". This expression does not indicate that what is referred to instantiates two universals, but one is tempted to suggest that it instantiates a single universal in a particular way or to a particular degree. But this, as " universal " was originally defined, is nonsense.

Thus the attempt to explain genuine thought by reference to universals involves us in one of two unexpected and disquieting consequences. We are obliged either to introduce such enigmatical notions as degrees of instantiation and relational universal-cum-particulars, which are as puzzling as the original problem left unexplained ; or to deny that comparative adjectives and such expressions as " nearly a . . .", and so on, can be more than noises. At best, the system of explanation is only a partial success. It assumed that universals were things of such a kind that particulars either instantiated them, or not ; but this proves to have been a simplification.

These, though, are merely peripheral difficulties. Hitherto an utterance has been described as genuinely expressing thought when " based on " the awareness of an appropriate universal. The central problem is to discover how, if at all, the utterance of verbal noises can be so based. It may be true that before a word can be used in genuine thought, even in such an utterance as " this is red ", the object of which the assertion is made must be recognized in some way as more than " merely particular " ; and it may be true, moreover, that the supplementation required is for the speaker to become aware of the object as an instance of the appropriate universal. But at this point an assumption has been made : that when it has once been said that the appropriate universal must be apprehended, then the problem of how verbal symbols can have meaning and enter into genuine thought, has been solved.

The assumption which is made is really twofold. First, it is assumed that every word *names* a single entity ; and second, that the relation between the general word (like red) and the entity which it names is diaphanously clear, and requires no explanation or discussion of any sort. When our attention is drawn to the apprehension of universals as something which from time to time accompanies the utterance of verbal noises, we shall need no explanation of how this apprehension makes the utterances more than mere noises. It is enough to know that universals were concurrently apprehended, and that these were their names.

This assumption is most remarkable. The relation of naming is in fact both complex and puzzling ; it is far from possessing such complete and convenient simplicity. Perhaps one can understand how a certain verbal noise could mean a particular object, as the hull of a ship means that its keel is there too, or as a thaw means burst pipes, or in some similar way. But it is hard to see how a certain momentary noise can mean an enduring object, by being its name, so that making the noise can mean the object in a genuinely thinking and cognitive manner. Indeed, it is doubtful if the relation between a proper name, and that object which it names, is really a relation of meaning at all. To say that " Jones " means Jones, or even worse, that it has Jones for its meaning, has absurd consequences. Does it not, for example, imply that the meaning of " Jones " is six feet tall, or fond of cheese ? If there are dangers of this kind connected with words naming physical objects, there are probably more serious ones connected with the general words which are supposed to name universals, and to be given meaning through doing so.

The manner in which a verbal utterance can be *based on* apprehension of some universal, in such a way that this foundation makes it more than reflex, must consequently be analysed in detail. The claim that this is possible because the verbal symbol names the universal must be put to the test. Let us take a particular example. Suppose that someone is shown a patch of colour, and on noticing it, says " red ". The theory says that if his utterance is appropriate to the colour, the following processes have occurred. First he perceives the particular colour, but apprehends it as more than merely particular; he apprehends it as instantiating the known colour-universal redness. Then he expresses this apprehension by using the symbol " red " to make an assertion. It would of course be impossible to identify these two processes, to say that apprehending the universal simply consisted in using the symbol. The first process has been introduced to explain how the second comes about, or rather to explain how on the given occasion it came about in a certain way and so was intelligent; and it would be nonsense to explain how an act or process had a certain quality, by asserting that it occurred. The awareness or apprehension, and the utterance, are necessarily two separate events, and the cogency of the whole theory depends on the relation between them.

But before examining this relation it is essential to recognize that there is no single entity which is the name of anything which has a name; no single entity which is always and everywhere produced when that thing is named. If this were so, the relation of naming might be a relatively simple one-one relation. The particular noise or mark, however, which constitutes the utterance of a symbol on a particular occasion, is never the reappearance of something which has occurred before and may occur again. It is a particular event, as individual and unique as a

hiccough, or a cat, or a comma. To use the " same word "
again, in the sense in which that is possible, is to produce
another noise or mark which is always numerically different, and usually different in quality, from the former.
Tuesday's words are not Monday's words reappearing;
they are as fresh as Tuesday's rain. Every day, perhaps,
the same dinner gong is beaten with the same stick, but
every day there is a new clang. If the butler calls " dinner "
instead, it is always the same butler, but never in the same
sense the same word. Whenever a word of a particular
" type " is used, a fresh " token ", a new particular, is
created ; and although this particular sound or mark may
in some sense be the name of, or signify one universal, it is
necessarily an instance of some other.

There are no names in ordinary language for the
universals of which particular verbal noises or marks are
instances, but for this discussion some method of naming
them must be invented. *Redness*, we are told, is the
universal of which particular red patches are instances ;
let us say that particular sounds or marks of the form " red "
are instances of the universal " *red* "-ness. The particular
sounds or marks " redness " and " ' red '-ness " are of course
instances of yet further universals, but fortunately it
will be unnecessary to name them too. This additional
terminology will make it easier to analyse the relation
between becoming aware of a universal instantiated in
some particular, and producing a sound or mark which is
its name. How does this particular " red " come into mind,
and how is its arrival related to awareness of the universal ?

It cannot be suggested that when the coloured patch is
apprehended as an instance of redness, this particular
sound or mark " red " simply pops out of the mouth or
flows automatically from the pen. This claim would
merely assimilate genuine thought to the performances
of the slot machine or the electric bell after all ; and the
whole theory has been brought forward to show how there

is an essential difference. One might circumvent the difficulty by saying that the apprehension of a universal is a process of so distinctive a kind, that other processes which apparently succeed it in an automatic manner, really succeed it intelligently and as part of genuine thinking. But would such an assertion constitute progress towards understanding the nature of genuine thinking? Would it not be simply a refusal to discuss the crucial difficulty? It implies that apprehending a universal is a process of so remarkable a character, that it makes perfectly simple a sequence which would otherwise be exceedingly perplexing. But if we enquire more closely about it, we are told only that it is the sort of process which makes genuine thinking possible, but that further questions cannot or will not be answered. This is unsatisfactory. It is really no more than an assertion that genuine thinking is a form of magic. This may be true; but it is not the kind of answer we have been encouraged to expect. The argument is like that of a superstitious peasant who asserts that his apples have been cankered by the fairies; but if asked how fairies canker apples, accuses the questioner of stupidity, or sacrilege, or both.

If such a mixture of superstition and dogma is not accepted, the difficulty must be evaded in some other way. For it is impossible to be content with the theory that that noise which is regarded as the name of the universal "just happens", when certain stimulating conditions are satisfied, whatever these may be. If this were the course of events, then the utterance is reflex and automatic, whether the stimulating conditions are perceiving the particular as "merely particular", or apprehending the universal — however profuse and authentic this latter process may be. There is still a reflex stage in the whole sequence; all that the theory has done is to suggest that it occurs in a new place. But at the same time, it insists that reflex processes cannot possibly occur in genuine thinking ; and so it gives no explanation at all.

There is no escape from this dilemma by suggesting that apprehending the first universal (*i.e.* redness) leads directly to apprehending a second (*i.e.* " red "-ness), and that the resulting utterance is simply the production of an instance of this second universal, in a particular " red ". Sometimes, perhaps, apprehending one universal leads to apprehending another in such a way that the transition from the first to the second is a genuine thought-process. Perhaps the universals named by " colour " and " exten-sion ", or by " back " and " front ", could be so connected in thought ; for it might be argued that in some sense colour entails extension, and the existence of a front entails the existence of a back. Between these pairs of universals there may perhaps be a logical or intelligible connexion. But between, for example, redness, and that hitherto in-nominate universal which we have agreed to call " ' red '-ness " (instances of which occur in naming the former universal), there is no connexion of this kind. There is no connexion between them which is not conventional, *de facto*, and restricted to the English-speaking peoples. If so, however, they cannot be linked in the mind by tracing an entailment. They can only be connected by association ; and if the relation is conventional and *de facto*, the association is not a cognitive or thinking process, but a reflex. Redness can only bring " red "-ness into mind, as at other times it might bring whiteness and blueness. Once again, the theory moves the reflex step, but does not remove it. But since it insists that there can never be reflex steps in genuine thinking, its explanation simply evanesces.

An attempt might be made to defend the universal in another way. It might be admitted that the name-word (or alternatively, the universal of which an uttered name-word would be an instance) is brought to mind only by a reflex. The whole process, nevertheless, is a genuine sequence of thinking, because this reflex is critically and intelligently tested as soon as it occurs ; and although the original process was reflex, the critical testing is more than reflex.

If, however, it is suggested that this process of critical testing is a verbal process, the old difficulty reappears. In the situations analysed above, a particular patch of colour was said to have been apprehended as " more than merely particular ", and as in fact constituting an instance of redness. The utterance " red " to describe it is admittedly prompted by a reflex ; but the reflex is critically tested. What could constitute this process of testing ? It could not be some expression such as " ' red ' would be an instance of the right universal for describing this sensible particular " ; for " the-right-universal-for-describing-this-sensible-particular " is no unique, unchanging, and constantly reappearing entity, but a particular noise, as particular as a cat, or a comma, or a " red " ; no more than an instance of a universal, the name of which may be left to the reader. There might be no difficulty in applying it to the particular " red " purely by a reflex ; but if its application is to be genuine thinking, it needs to be critically tested just as much as the original description of the coloured patch by the utterance " red ". Could there be a second process of critical checking to validate the first, taking perhaps the verbal form " ' the-right- . . . -particular ' — a fair description in this case of the relation between sensible particular and verbal symbol " ? Is this not merely a third particular noise (or verbal image if thought silently), an instance merely of some third universal, whose name veritably defies contemplation ? Plainly, there is no means of avoiding an infinite regress ; and this is tantamount to admitting that no genuine explanation was really given of the original process.

Indeed, an attempt to extricate oneself from the initial

difficulties by having recourse to processes of critical checking has even more extravagant consequences than those discussed so far. The analysis given above is incomplete. Should the speaker have said "red" before he began the critical process, then the utterance itself would be a reflex, even were his subsequent thought to be promoted to the level of intelligence. The utterance can only manifest thought, if the testing precedes or concomitantly shepherds it. The speaker must first, therefore, reflect in terms somewhat like these: "'red' would be an instance . . . etc. . . . , so here goes: — ", and then follow this reflection by uttering the word "red". But the "red" in the reflection, and the "red" uttered, are two separate particulars, not one entity reappearing twice; and the second does not cease to have been a reflex utterance, merely because the first has already been critically approved. It needs to be validated by some further critical process, perhaps of the form ". . . which is an instance of the same universal as the previous 'red' occurring in my thought". This is a stratagem which only multiplies the difficulties. For in the first plan the utterance "red" remains a reflex; the critical checking follows it and therefore cannot change its status. In the second, the particular "red" which occurs in this critical process can only be connected with the particular "red" in the original critical process, through the mediation of still another process. Since this will necessarily include a "red", it will require a successor to validate it, and so on *ad infinitum*.

That such processes as these do not occur is so certain, that it seems unnecessary to argue that even if they did they would be futile. But to analyse these futilities in a verbal form serves one important purpose. It might have been suggested that critical processes of this kind actually did occur and were effective; but that they were not constituted by verbal thought, or indeed by any other type of imagery. This convenient *incognito*, however, rescues them from none of the formal difficulties analysed above in respect of verbal processes. For any mental process which critically validates any other, will necessarily consist of certain elements; and these must necessarily be particular, universal, both, or neither. But if this is admitted, non-verbal processes can serve no better than verbal. If their elements consist of an acquaintance with particulars, then they are useless; for it has already been shown that on this theory there can be no intelligent and non-reflex passage from one universal to an alien particular which succeeds it. If these processes have as their constituents an awareness of universals, they are useless because there can be no genuine movement in thought between two universals linked only by association. If the elements of these processes are both universal and particular, or are neither, then their nature is more obscure than that of the original sequence of thought which they were introduced to explain. They take us back to the realm of magic and dogma, which we had hoped to quit through their aid.

So much for the attempts to show that general words can occur in genuine thought, because they are connected with universals. It is interesting to note in addition that even had the theory survived examination, it would not have explained how using proper names could be more than a reflex. Some proper names are more or less descriptive, as, for example, when a large white borzoi dog is called " Snowdrift ". To some extent this is like the metaphorical use of a general word, drawing attention to certain of the dog's qualities, and asserting that he resembles other objects in various ways. If the theory of universals had explained anything, it might have explained, at least in part, how such names could be used intelligently. But other proper names entirely lack this descriptive element. If the white borzoi is called " Joey ", there may be no suggestion, in its use, that he resembles any of the boys, parrots, goldfish, or spaniels also called " Joey ". But it is impossible to explain how such a name can occur in genuine thought, if the only technique of explanation consists in showing that a word was used because the speaker recognized a certain particular as instantiating the universal which that word names. The use of a proper name involves nothing about universals. One does not assert that the white borzoi called " Joey " is of the same sort as other objects called " Joey " ; nor that it resembles other objects (like other white borzois) which in fact it does resemble ; nor that this appearance of a white borzoi called " Joey " instantiates the same universals as were instantiated by previous experiences of the same dog (for this may not be true). No assertion is being made about sorts, or resemblances, or universals. The statement asserts rather that the dog now perceived is the same dog as was formerly perceived ; and even if the expression " same dog " is analysed so that it refers to a class of particulars, the problem remains. For it must be a class of particulars quite differently constructed from the class of instances of one universal. A particular is a member of the latter class by virtue of resembling other particulars, but is a member of the former by virtue of different and complex relations, normally of spatial and temporal continuity.

This objection, like the others raised in this chapter, is not absolutely conclusive. One may override it by saying that there is an alternative and hitherto undiscussed theory which explains how using proper names is not necessarily reflex ; or by admitting that their use constitutes a reflex *lacuna* in the succession of genuine thought : or perhaps by some other device. One can always avoid an infinite regress, by asserting that the question which generates it cannot legitimately be raised in the given case ; or render nugatory an objection that one's theory creates exactly the same difficulties as it solves, by asserting as a dogma that the difficulties cannot exist in regard to it; or make extravagant consequences relatively acceptable, by the assertion that, after all, they follow from the only possible solution of a difficulty. The crucial point, however, is that when the theory was introduced, these consequences of it were not prominent. Had they been prominent, its initial plausibility would have been negligible. The supplementary devices whereby we cling to a pseudo-explanation attract us only because we once supposed that the explanation was genuine, and remain unwilling to abandon the illusion.

The discussion so far has aimed simply at proving that the apprehension of particulars as instances of some universal cannot explain how general words have meanings and so how genuine thought is possible. No attempt was made to prove that universals do not exist in any sense; or that particulars do not instantiate them; or that they are not apprehended in particulars. It will be sufficient if they are seen not to answer the purpose for which they were introduced.

This type of restriction on the aim of the discussion becomes even more important if we turn to the conceptualist theory. That too has its account to offer of how words have meaning. The account, as before, is that words are the names of single entities; but this time these entities are " mental contents " pure and simple. These contents, or concepts, or as they are sometimes called, " meanings ", are the real material of thought; they constitute it and are its life. Words are significant only because they express them. A quotation from a modern psychologist will illustrate this theory in sharp outline :

> Separate parts [of thought] are sometimes, but by no means always, provided with linguistic signs to enable us to make ourselves intelligible to ourselves and to others. The stream of thought and the phonic stream are both

split up into corresponding systems, so that the ideas signified and the system of signifiers more or less correspond.[1]

References to " meaning " and " meanings " are common in modern philosophical writings. Miss Susan Stebbing says, " only words or symbols can have *meaning* ".[2] C. I. Lewis writes :

> It is obvious that common meanings do transcend . . . individual differences of perception and imagery. We use language to convey thought. If language really conveys anything, then there must be something which is identical in your mind and in mine when we understand each other. And if our thought is objective and not merely a report of introspection, then what is identical in our two minds must also be somehow germane to that objective reality. . . .[3]

And earlier :

> The question, how meaning *can* be objective and shared, when the psychological states which are bearers of this meaning are separate existences and not even identical in their qualitative content, is one of the important problems of meaning . . . that meanings have this sort of objectivity, is a fundamental assumption of science or of any other intellectual exercise . . . there must be meanings which are common to minds when they co-operate. . . . On the other hand, I see no reason for resigning the problem of meanings to the psychologist as his exclusive affair, especially as he . . . must begin by assuming their existence. The meaning must be somehow identified before it can be correlated with behaviour or motor-set or anything else.[4]

Miss Susanne Langer [5] utilizes the word frequently : " It is necessary to examine . . . that which makes *symbols* out of anything — out of marks on paper, the little squeaks

---

[1] Charles Fox, *The Mind and its Body* (1931), p. 121.
[2] *A Modern Introduction to Logic* (1933), Appendix A.   Italics are as in the original in all passages quoted.
[3] *Mind and the World Order* (1929), p. 73.   [4] *Ibid.* pp. 69-72.
[5] *Philosophy in a New Key* (1942).

and grunts we interpret as ' words ', or bended knees —
the quality of *meaning*, in its several aspects and forms ".[1]
" Meaning has both a logical and a psychological aspect " : [2]
" Metaphysics is, like every philosophical pursuit, the
study of *meanings* ".[3] " No symbol is exempt from the
office of logical formulation, of *conceptualizing* what it
conveys; however simple its import, or however great,
this import is a *meaning*, and therefore an element for
understanding." [4]

Mr. Belgion discusses how words are connected with
meanings in another way.[5] In most of our conversation,
he suggests, words occur without " precise " or " careful
and definite " meanings. We repeat stock jokes and
phrases, and we talk without thinking, like a parrot. But
sometimes we " express with words a fully clear and conscious meaning of our own ".[6] When this occurs the
words and the meanings must beyond dispute be two, and
separate. If even under these circumstances it could not
be said that the words had meanings, there could be no
way of distinguishing such occasions from occasions when
word-noises are simply mechanical counters. " There is
the positive difficulty . . . of both apprehending a meaning
and finding words for it. This positive difficulty is the
greater that having a meaning, and having words with
which to give it a local habitation and a name, are two
distinct things. They must be two, or we could not use
words, as I have shown us to use them so much, without
meaning." [7] The same sharp distinction is a commonplace
in every sort of writing about symbols and about language.
One finds Eric Partridge, for example, referring to " mental
conceptions and the words that express them " ; [8] and

---

[1] *Op. cit.* p. 52. Miss Langer, it should be noted, later asserts that
meaning is not a quality.
[2] *Ibid.* p. 53. [3] *Ibid.* p. 85. [4] *Ibid.* p. 97.
[5] M. Belgion, " *The Human Parrot* " *and other Essays* (Oxford, 1931).
[6] *Ibid.* p. 16. [7] *Ibid.* p. 17.
[8] *The World of Words* (1938), p. 147.

in an essay on " Meaning and Reality " J. F. Crawford writes " all meaning . . . must be carried by some symbol ".[1]

These quotations from many different writers working at different levels of philosophical sophistication give an impression of the conceptualist theory and the uses to which it is put. It is doubtful whether any other single piece of philosophizing is so widely accepted, or so deeply embedded in the thought and writings of philosophers and non-philosophers alike. These quotations collectively illustrate the main contours of the theory. Those from Fox, Belgion, Partridge, and Crawford show how thoughts and words are conceived as forming two distinct sequences, the one depending on the other. That from Miss Stebbing emphasizes how meaning and symbols are essentially connected. Those from Miss Langer illustrate the reputed identity between meanings and concepts ; and those from C. I. Lewis, how communication is believed to involve some identical content of meaning present in the minds of speaker and hearer, how this identical content is not very blatantly present, and how " if our thought is object-ive ", it must be " germane to . . . reality ". What will now be examined is the theory of concepts as a whole ; these quotations have been given to illustrate its main features, and no attempt will be made to examine the views of the individual writers or the divergencies between them.

On this theory it is not at first sight easy to see how words and their meanings are related to objects. The relation is secured, however, by giving the concept a dual rôle ; it is to function as both the universal instantiated by the particular object (say, the red patch) and the meaning of the word. The particular is related to the concept by instantiating it, and the word is related because it has the concept as its meaning. This identification of

---

[1] *Essays in Philosophy* (edited T. V. Smith and W. K. Wright, Open Court Co., 1929), p. 86.

D

what the particular instantiates, and what the word means, is rarely noticed and never proved; but whether it could be proved will not now be discussed.[1]

In one way the theory is more secure than that of Cook-Wilson. If the concept is a mental content, then it is not to be expected that it should also actually exist in any particular which instantiates it — indeed, this would probably be nonsense. But the initial difficulties which confronted a realist or *in re* theory, arose because this theory was obliged to confess that the universal was either really present and so instantiated in the particular; or not present and so not instantiated.[2] A plain " yes " or a plain " no " was all that could ever be said. This simple choice did not accord with the complexity of the facts. A conceptualist theory, however, can easily define " being an instance of ", in some more complex way, which makes it possible for particulars to be better or worse instances, and instantiate the concept more or less fully. Should this be done, those difficulties called " peripheral " above will be avoided.

But this is a triviality. For the crucial objections made above to the *in re* theory apply equally to conceptualism; and in addition it has certain difficulties of its own. The difficulties peculiar to this theory arise from the very device which rescued it from the quandary in which the *in re* theory found itself, faced with varying degrees of instantiation. There was at least no problem, for this theory, of how particular and universal could be connected by the mind. The universal was actually present in its instance. Acquaintance with the particular was *ipso facto* awareness of the universal; the particular was only recognized as particular because at the same time it was recognized as more than particular. But in the concep-

---

[1] See, however, J. L. Austin, *Proceedings of the Aristotelian Society*, Supp. Vol. 18, pp. 84-88, where it is disproved.
[2] See above, p. 18.

tualist theory this simplicity disappears. There is nothing present in the particular but its particular qualities; and the only link these have with the outside world, is that each particular quality is related to a mental content, a concept which is virtually stored in someone's mind.

Now it may easily be possible to define the relation between existent particular and mental content, so that the one can instantiate the other in varying degrees. But the problem is to define it so that the two may actually be linked in the mind by a process of genuine thought, and not a mere reflex. This it is extremely difficult to do. One cannot say that particular and universal are related by resemblance; partly because resemblance is the typical foundation of reflex and habitual transitions, but chiefly for another reason. It is difficult to see how a red patch can (in any but irrelevant respects such as origin, size, etc.) resemble anything but another red patch. But if the concept is also a red patch, it must be a sort of image; and the theory denies that concepts are in any way like images. If it is not an image, and if even so the genuine passage in thought from particular to concept depends on a relation of resemblance, it must be a resemblance of some peculiar and hitherto unexplained kind. The problem may be solved instead by saying simply that the relation between particular and mental concept is such that it makes possible an intelligent transition from sensing the particular to contemplating the universal. In other words, the relation " being an instance of " itself provides for genuine passage in thought. The disadvantage is that this assertion is only a dogmatic claim that the relation is magic.

The conceptualist and *in re* theories taken together introduce no less than four entities in describing the process of describing a particular as an act of genuine thought; and it is justifiable to list all four, because the two theories, though quite incompatible, are frequently combined, one being used at one time, the other at another. First there is the sensible particular, then the universal which it instantiates, then the meaning of the descriptive word, and finally the verbal utterance itself. The *in re* theory sharply distinguished universals from meanings, and in consequence " being an instance of " was not given the flexibility which it needed as a foundation for the actual use of words. The conceptualist theory identifies universal and meaning, and thereby can secure this flexibility of instantiation; but as the price of this gain, the connexion between meaning and particular is either entirely arbitrary and reflex, or entirely mysterious and occult. These are the " peripheral " difficulties peculiar to the conceptualist theory.

The crucial difficulties, however, are those which ruined the *in re* theory. This could not show why uttering the word was an intelligent sequel to apprehending the universal; and the conceptualist theory cannot show why it is an intelligent sequel to conceiving the concept. This remains true, even if by " concept " is meant a fusion of what the particular instantiates, and what the word means. The objection against the *in re* theory was twofold, that the central process was either a reflex process from apprehended universal to uttered noise, or a reflex process from one universal (redness) to another (" red "-ness), between which there was only an arbitrary and *de facto* association. The same twofold difficulty faces the conceptualist theory. What is uttered is still a particular noise; and what link can exist between a concept or meaning, and a noise, save one that is automatic and reflex? Evasion by appealing to critical and intelligent checking will create the original problems and regresses once again. On the other hand, there could be a word to describe an utterance like " red ", for this is as much a particular as the original patch of colour; and if the utterance were described (*e.g.* by a second utterance " that was ' red ' ", like " that was

G sharp "), then the description would itself have a meaning and be the expression of a concept. Let us, as before, call this second concept or meaning " ' red '-ness ", as in discussing the *in re* theory we called the second universal. The connexion between these two concepts or meanings would necessarily be as conventional, local, and *de facto*, as that alleged to hold between the universals. But for the conceptualist theory as for the *in re* theory, reflex steps based on mere habit are alien to the genuine processes of thought. Both theories lose what cogency they seemed to possess, because they reintroduce, and rely upon, transitions of the very type they ostracize.

It should be emphasized once again, perhaps, that the purpose of this discussion was not to prove that there are no mental contents which may conveniently be termed concepts or meanings. Nor was it to prove that " mental life " consists only of images, or indeed to make any assertions about the constituents or nature of consciousness at all. But words like " concept " and " meaning " were not introduced purely for descriptive purposes by those who advocated the theories discussed. They were introduced to make a hierarchical classification of mental life, and to show how some mental processes (such as using words) could sometimes have a distinctive and indeed distinguished character. They were introduced to explain how verbal sequences and utterances could sometimes constitute processes of genuine and intelligent thought, and be more than merely reflex, more than " talking without thinking ". The present discussion seeks only to show that the explanation is unsuccessful ; either it merely transplants the problem, or it disposes of it by dogma and by appeals to magic.

This restriction is particularly important, because a good deal of empirical evidence has been collected to show that we are sometimes, as the investigators have themselves expressed it, " acquainted with meanings ".[1]   Thus it appears at first sight as if there is empirical confirmation of the presence of meanings in thought, whatever may be believed as to their efficacy.   One of the central doctrines of this group of psychologists was that, in Spearman's words, " thought could exist without either images or verbal representations " ; there could be " long stretches of thought without any detectable images ".   Speaking of his own typical state of consciousness while thinking intently, Spearman says, " such a general course of cognition as that of the present writer, surging on like a deep, dark, formless sea, and almost unconcerned with the meagre sentience incoherently twittering on a higher level of cognitive intensity, may be contrasted with the mind that can describe itself as follows : — ".[2]   He then quotes an autobiographical passage from Titchener,[3] who is content to describe his own thinking entirely in terms of imagery.

Spearman drew from Aveling's experimental work, and was himself one of the subjects in it.   Aveling taught a small group of persons to understand and use a group of " words " invented for the purpose, by associating these constantly with sets of pictures, all of the same sort of object or event.   The subjects were asked to report, from introspection, how they understood these words, once learnt, in the absence of the pictures, and to describe the processes of completing sentences or answering questions in which they occurred.

Aveling did not simply deny that thought consisted only of images and inner speech.   He asserted, and this was his crucial point, that the imageless constituents which his subjects reported were the vital thread and explaining

[1] See, for example, C. Spearman, *The Nature of Intelligence* (1923), chap. xii ; or F. Aveling, *The Consciousness of the Universal* (1912), *passim*.

[2] *Op. cit.* p. 182.

[3] E. B. Titchener, *Lectures on the Experimental Psychology of the Thought-Process* (1909), pp. 9-10.

factor in thinking. In other words, he identified the empirically observable elements of consciousness investigated by him with the meanings or concepts already believed on philosophical grounds to make thought really thought. In the various processes of understanding the " nonsense-words ", once they had been given significance by association with the pictures, he distinguished various stages of emancipation from dependence on imagery. At first, there was an awareness or understanding of the meaning only when some relevant image had already arrived; as familiarity increased, awareness of the meaning, the crucial stage of enlightenment, preceded the image, which merely trailed along behind it, or might indeed not occur at all; ultimately, awareness of the meaning was no more than a glow or aura which enveloped the word-noise.

Aveling is emphatic, however, that word and meaning are distinct. He says:

> Introspection shows that this meaning is present as a purely ideational concept. Though " carried by " the word, it is not the word; which was, in our experiments, present as a sensorial (visual) stimulus. This is not only clear from the fact that the word meant something other than itself; and that the meaning was an imageless presence of " object " to consciousness. It is also evinced by the fact that the particular stage of the " growth of meaning " under discussion is the last of a process in which this imageless knowledge gradually comes to be " carried by " the word.[1]

He sums up his general conclusion in the following way:

> We would submit, then, that our data have enabled us to establish with regard to this matter the point that perception and reproduction involve concepts in adult human consciousness. These, we have shown, are to be found revived, without the intervention of visual imagery, by a nonsense word with which they have been arbitrarily associated. And we have shown, further, that where such imagery is present, this also involves the presence of concepts. This

[1] *Op. cit.* p. 107.

would appear to point clearly to the conclusion that without what we have called conceptual abstraction, human perception and reproduction cannot be explained.[1]

Aveling thought he had provided empirical confirmation of the philosophical theory that concepts are the bases of genuine thought, and are the meanings which lend significance to word-noises.

Aveling's descriptive work is often interesting. But it does not lend support to the conceptualist theory examined in this chapter, because the mental states which he observed cannot be identified with the " concepts " and " meanings " referred to in that theory; and unless this identification is possible, his empirical and these theoretical studies are unrelated. It is not difficult to show that the mental states observed have no bearing on the theoretical arguments about " meanings ", if one remembers how these arguments employed the term. In them, the meaning was what gave a certain word its significance. Without it, the word would have been a mere noise. It had a constant significance because always linked to the same meaning; and had it ever been linked with a different meaning, it would have had a different significance. Finally, since it would be nonsense to say that someone used a word in intelligent thought but was not aware of its meaning, the meaning was necessarily present whenever the word was more than a mere noise. Thus the linkage with a certain " meaning " or concept was a sufficient condition of the word's having a particular significance; and was also a necessary condition.

But it is indisputable that these conditions do not hold of the introspectible experiences studied by Aveling. First, it is exceedingly improbable that such an experience would be sufficient for genuinely understanding and using a word. Let us suppose that there is a certain exhaustively describable mental experience enjoyed by a certain person

[1] *Op. cit.* pp. 115-116.

in understanding a particular word on a certain occasion. Could it be thought that anyone who had precisely this mental experience — which, one must remember, is an imageless experience — would " know the meaning " in the sense required by the conceptualist theory ? Could it be supposed that anyone, in whom was reproduced (perhaps by telepathy) precisely the reader's experience when he understood " imageless " in the last sentence, would then know the meaning of " imageless " ? If so, he would at least be able to invent a word to express that meaning; and he would use this invented word precisely as the reader would use " imageless ", and with precisely the same insight. Indeed, if his thinking were of the deep-sea variety, he could privately employ the meaning of " imageless " henceforth, without further ado. In this way one could learn the meanings of every word for an empirical quality or type of real object, without recourse to experience. A blind man could come to know the meaning of " red " simply by enjoying the observable mental experience of an artist using that word in (careful) conversation ; he could not only dispense with any image of red which might have been in the mind of the other, but would even find it convenient to do so. These possibilities seem very remote. But unless they are accepted, one must admit that Aveling was not investigating the " meanings " relevant to the theory.

Aveling's own evidence, however, shows conclusively that the experiences which he studied are not necessary to understanding the words, or using them in genuine thought. The " meaning " (or concept) as it appears in the theory, must occur whenever the word is more than a mere noise. It is a factor common not only to all those occasions on which the word is used by one speaker, but to all the occasions of using it, by every speaker.[1] Had Aveling investigated " meaning " in this sense, then he

[1] Compare the quotations from C. I. Lewis, p. 31.

should have discovered such a common and constant mental experience.   But his evidence shows instead that, even with one subject, the experience of understanding a particular word varies from time to time, especially as the word becomes a more familiar part of one's vocabulary. It would be very difficult to prove that the mental states of two subjects understanding one word were either exactly similar or indisputably different.   But everything in Aveling's evidence which suggests anything in this respect, suggests that the differences in experience between different people are very considerable.   The only exception appeared to be, as one would expect, when the word had become so familiar that it was difficult to speak of any " experience of understanding " at all.   By this time, it seemed, a casual oblivion had descended on those for whom thought was a deep sea, as much as on those for whom it was, presumably, a flashing stream.

Aveling's evidence, therefore, does not confirm the conceptualist theory at all; the observations which he studied were unrelated to it.   Indeed, the paragraph in which he summed up his conclusions affords unconscious confirmation of the present argument.   His mode of expression chances to confirm the claim that reference to concepts cannot explain genuine thought, though it may assert dogmatically that certain processes are instances of it. In the passage quoted he says [1] that concepts are to be " found revived " by a nonsense - word " arbitrarily " associated with them.   This is a tacit confession that the movement in thought from word to concept, and indeed also from concept to word, is a reflex movement.   Aveling's phraseology has inadvertently betrayed the speciousness of his theory.   It is curious and unfortunate also that he did not notice a similarity between learning the meanings of his " nonsense "-words and acquiring habits.

There is no escaping the conclusion that the presence

[1] See above, p. 39, the second passage quoted.

of a " concept " or " meaning " cannot be confirmed by observation ; it is simply an entity whose presence is both required and demonstrated by a theory. The theory, in brief, says that genuine thought occurs, and that this would be impossible unless we had awareness of concepts. Therefore this awareness occurs. But there is no means of supplementing this knowledge of what concepts are like. If the theory is to achieve its purpose, indeed, concepts must have properties which can only be described as magical ; and which, because they need to defy the results of observation, must also defy the process. Whatever observation discovers seems to vary from time to time and from person to person ; but the meaning must always be present and never vary, because its presence is necessitated by what occurs. We are assured that this it is which makes possible the genuine thought we observe, but otherwise its nature is unknown ; it is a wholly explicative entity. It is introduced merely to explain. Attempts to be better acquainted with it destroy its uneasy efficacy.

CHAPTER III

SIGNS AND SYMBOLS

THE established accounts of how words come to have their special status therefore seem unsatisfactory. Instead of proposing an alternative account, however, we shall pursue the enquiry by asking what exactly are the boundaries of that part of human behaviour which makes such an account necessary. In this enquiry certain assumptions, frequently made, will be avoided. We have agreed that if symbols are used so as really to have meanings, then they occur in behaviour which is not mechanical but intelligent ; but it is frequently taken for granted, either that all intrinsically intelligent behaviour is symbol-using behaviour, or else that even the use of symbols is only intelligent by derivation from anterior mental processes. We shall make no assumptions about the coincidence or otherwise of the boundaries of behaviour using symbols and intelligent behaviour ; we shall merely begin by examining what happens when individuals react to particulars which have meaning in some sense, but admittedly not in the sense which words do when genuinely used. These particulars are normally called signs. By this means we take the simple forms first, and when their scope is fully known it will be time to ask what account must be given of whatever they omit.

One event or object, if a sign, is always the sign of another ; and to say that it is a sign of another, is to say that the first means the second, or that its significance is the second. The realm of non-linguistic signs is much wider than that of language; in fact, any two events or objects may be signs each of the other, provided that they regularly occur together. This regular concomitance is manifested by whatever is connected more or less closely in a causal pattern. A cause can be a sign of its effect, as the crack of the pistol can mean, for someone unable to see the race, that the runners have started. An effect can be a sign of its cause, as waving trees are a sign of the wind. One effect of a cause can be the sign of another, which may be simultaneous with it but less easily observed, or subsequent. For example, the texture of snow may be a sign that the ice will not bear skating, and the colour of a leaf, a sign that soon it will fall to the ground.

But it is incomplete to speak merely of one event being a sign of another; we must refer to some individual who " grasps " or " knows " or at least is " responsive " to the meaning of the sign, and who interprets it or at least reacts in some way to its significance. Were this implication not present, " being a sign of " would mean the same as " being causally associated with ". This interpretation or reaction would be impossible if there were not a regular concomitance between sign and signified, a regularity which need not be entirely without exception, but must be appreciable. It must be sufficiently marked to induce a corresponding regularity of behaviour on the part of whoever or whatever interprets the event as a sign. At the simplest level, we interpret a sign when, on observing it, we behave somewhat as we would on observing what it signifies. This is why it is legitimate to say that events and conditions have a significance for animals. High wind makes the cattle seek shelter as if from rain; rabbits dive into their holes when the birds squawk in alarm, but not when they sing; a dog wags his tail if his master takes up his hat. Even plants that grow towards the light, or curl up their leaves to catch insects which alight on them, are behaving similarly.

With these " natural signs " there is neither need nor scope for any form of agreement between those who react to them. It would be impossible to agree that dark clouds should be a sign of anything other than coming rain, and animals which react to the significances of their environment do not agree as to what it shall be, but are simply subject to its influence. Other signs are more or less artificial; they do not occur naturally, but are introduced with a more or less deliberate intention of conveying information or inducing certain behaviour. Red and green lights indicate that a road is closed or open ; a figure on the flyleaf of a book means that the book costs so many shillings ; a visiting-card left without comment or message means that an acquaintance has called ; a ring on a certain finger is a sign that a woman is married. But there need not be any explicit convention for the meaning of these signs to be understood. The activities of one man comprise part of the environment of another ; and, without any convention, his behaviour can be interpreted as significant of something else, provided only that it occurs with it more or less as regularly as does a natural sign with what it signifies.

A very large part of practical life consists in appreciating the significance of signs like these, and in reacting to them in one way or another. From the very first moment of waking, one's behaviour tends to be determined continuously by the meaning of one occurrence or another. Throughout the day, observed natural and artificial signs, between which there is no sharp distinction, are indications of what exists or has occurred unobserved. One is " alive to a situation " when one reacts to the significance of the signs within it, which mean something about what is outside it.

The terminology of " stimulus ", " response ", and " conditioning " will be used to analyse the process of reacting to a sign ; and the range of behaviour which can be described adequately in these terms must be ascertained with some care, for the guiding question, after all, is of what part of human activity falls outside that range, and what such activity is like. The typical pattern of response to a stimulus and of conditioning such a response is well known. Certain unlearned responses appear in animals and humans from birth ; a dog, for example, salivates when he is shown a piece of food, and this response is never learnt. But it can be gradually transferred from the stimulus of the food itself, to something else which regularly accompanies it. Behaving, however, in a manner more or less appropriate to one event, on observing another which regularly accompanies it, was what we accepted above as the simplest form of interpreting a sign, or of " knowing " its meaning. The second event has become a sign of the first. In wild life the secondary stimulus is always a " natural " sign ; but when animals are experimented upon or taught tricks, it is more or less artificial. This distinction will prove of importance later.

The process of learning does not consist merely in the transference of unlearned or innate responses to new stimuli ; it involves the multiplication, modification, and lapsing of responses by a variety of methods and to a very high degree of complexity. But all the time, it is possible to use the sign-meaning terminology and the stimulus-response terminology together. " Transferring a response " to a new stimulus is another way of describing the most rudimentary form of interpreting a sign. The secondary stimulus is a sign of, and means, the original stimulus ; that this is true for the animal is proved by his behaviour having been so conditioned by his experience, that he reacts to the first in a manner appropriate to the second.

To some extent, certainly, the behaviour of humans can be described in terms of stimulus and response, and illustrates the conditioning of responses to new stimuli. At first, perhaps, we put on a coat or seek shelter when the rain begins to fall; but when we have learnt from experience, we do so when the threatening clouds appear. This change need not be thought out step by step. But humans, like animals, sometimes transfer their responses in a purely spontaneous manner. A baby who learns first to stretch out his hands to his food, learns later to stretch them out to his mother. A boxing novice defends himself from his opponent's punch, when he sees it coming; but a veteran's defence begins when he notices certain movements of the other's eyes or feet. A motorist learns to slow down at night, when all he can see is the glow of another car's lights over the brow of a hill. He may even say that he slows down " automatically " on such an occasion.

Furthermore, human activity sometimes involves a responsiveness to natural signs which is contrary to the most conspicuous features of our environment. A pilot learns to respond to the stimulus of the sleeve, although at the height of his aeroplane the wind itself may be in a different direction. A motorist will slow down at a road sign which means a steep hill, even if he cannot see the hill. The sign itself may take the form of a black right-angled triangle, or marks of the form " STEEP HILL ". Either will suffice if it occurs regularly enough in this sort of environment. Similarly, he will stop if the policeman shouts " stop ! " as readily as if he sees a warning light or a barricade. A soldier can be taught or drilled to execute complex multiple operations on the stimulus of a single complex command. There is no reason, at this level, for distinguishing vocal and non-vocal stimuli, or uttered cries, and uttered words such as words of command. A vocal noise, whether a word or not, is a single physical event just like the sound of a bell or the flash of a light; and it is perfectly natural that responses should be conditioned to it, if it is a sign of something else, in just the same way.

Perhaps it is impossible to say why response to stimuli, whether verbal or non-verbal, occurs at all; or why a particular response can be transferred from one stimulus to another. But an explanation can be given of why certain responses develop and not others; or why a response is transferred to one stimulus and not to another. As a preliminary, however, a correspondence should be noted between a learned or conditioned response and a habit. To say that a certain response has been conditioned, implies that the subject exhibits an abiding tendency to behave in a certain way, whenever an event of a certain kind falls within his experience. This is equivalent to saying that the subject has acquired a habit of behaving in a particular way when he finds himself in a particular kind of situation. Just as habits are acquired and also lapse, so responses are inhibited as well as developed and transferred. The history of an organism is one in which, continuously, certain patterns of behaviour develop, and others disappear. The two sorts of change cannot be rigidly separated, because a pattern of behaviour usually disappears, simply in that the organism tends more and more to behave in some other way. But an account of how behaviour develops must do justice to both these aspects of the life-history of an organism.

At first it seems as if one could account for exactly what habits are developed and of these which are retained and which abandoned, by speaking of successful behaviour. Behaviour, we should say, is successful if it satisfies desire; and habits which tend to bring success are more and more deeply implanted, while those which bring ill-success disappear. This suggestion, however, borrows a terminology developed to describe the most self-conscious and deliberate behaviour of human adults, and uses it for much simpler organisms. It is difficult to say that, for example, mice have desires, or to prove that they have this or that desire, except on the evidence of the very

E

behaviour which the desire has been introduced to explain. Similar difficulties arise if one says that habits tend to become rooted if they bring pleasure. Consequently, the best method is to start with the details. For any particular type of organism it is possible to specify certain conditions, of which it is true that behaviour which regularly tends to produce them becomes confirmed into a habit, and behaviour with contrary results is abandoned. As these optimum conditions are more and more fully reached, the restlessness of the organism decreases to nil. Whether they are said to be objects of desire or to produce pleasure is of little importance, though the favourable conditions for animals are largely also favourable conditions for human beings; and with human beings are often connected with " desire " and " pleasure " which can be given meaning independently. For brevity's sake, however, activity which tends to produce such conditions will sometimes be referred to simply as " successful activity ".

Some examples of how certain behaviour-processes are confirmed, and others neutralized, will emphasize two important points. A dog that is given its dinner if it begs or whines, but not if it barks, will develop a habit of begging or whining, and the tendency to bark on such occasions will disappear. If it succeeds in getting through a fence at one place, and fails at every other place, it will form the habit of going directly to the gap and ignoring the rest of the fence. The first successful attempt may be the result of persistent trial and error, or may be because the dog follows its master. Cattle and sheep can also form a habit of going straight to a gap in the fence; and an individual sheep might find its way through in the first instance simply by following the others, and imitating them. Imitation does not require a conscious decision to imitate, based on some insight into what will bring success; it is not too sophisticated a process to assist in the rudimentary forming of habits. It is itself a habit, induced by past successes.

This is the first of the two points mentioned above, and it leads to the second. Chance movements of the mouth and tongue, and imitation of the noises made by others, together produce the earliest vocal noises in children. In consequence, the stimulus-response pattern is as adequate to the development of verbal responses to stimuli as to that of responses to verbal stimuli. That is to say, the growth of habits of using language can be described in the same terms as responding to its use by others. So far, there is no reason to set vocal or verbal behaviour in a class by itself. A child can acquire habits of using his hands, or of using his mouth to make cries (perhaps of delight or anger), or of using his mouth to make verbal noises. There is no need to make a distinction between activities of these three kinds. Each equally results in the occurrence of certain physical events, and one terminology can equally be used for them all.

By now it is clear that habits in which a word or set of words is either stimulus, or response, can be formed in the same way as other non-verbal habits. Nor is there anything which would prevent habits of responding to or using a word, in the absence of the sort of situation with which originally it was associated. A word-noise which occurs outside such a context can have significance, at the least, like a dark cloud which is a sign of rain still to come. The parallel, indeed, is close, since a response to the dark cloud alone may have been acquired because sometimes cloud and rain are perceived simultaneously; and a word may be responded to, though it occurs in the absence of its object, because they occurred together often enough for some appropriate response to be transferred. Conversely, one may say " a rose is . . . red ", though no rose or other red object is present, because there already exists a verbal habit of conjoining the first and the second expressions. To claim that such sentences can only be completed if the mind is working with the concept of colour, would be as absurd as to suggest that a lion could only pounce on an antelope if it had already decided it was on a hunting expedition.

It might be argued that this account of hearing a word-noise in the absence of the sort of object which it indicates is incomplete, because there often is an under-standing, but no behaviour which can constitute the response. But "understanding" is an ambiguous term; we have not yet decided whether a distinction between "hearing and responding" and "really understanding" ought sometimes to be made, or not. The point at issue is only that a response could occur; and that there is no need to distinguish between verbal and non-verbal stimuli, in either degree or manner of efficacy. The response might not always occur, admittedly; if only because several stimuli may be operative together, and one be neutralized by the other. But this applies to verbal and non-verbal stimuli alike.

It is important to discover what are the limits of complexity which could be reached, if responding to and using language were developed only by the elaboration of verbal habits. Certainly whole sentences could, in this rudimentary sense, be used and understood as easily as single words. One may question indeed whether an individual whose linguistic equipment was only of this kind would possess any technique for distinguishing between words and sentences. Sentence-noises would seem to him only like prolonged and elaborate word-noises; and these like fragmentary sentence-noises. He could develop habits of uttering and receiving either equally well; and would simply not be sophisticated enough to think of dissecting sentences into their constituent parts. Further, his habitual equipment might easily be such that he could utter a whole series of sentences; and it might be true that the series was one of logical entailments in a single deductive argument. But his behaviour would be correctly described by saying that each part of the series of word-noises which he uttered was a response to the stimulus of what he had already said. He would doubtless have had originally to acquire the series by imitation from the spoken or written word. But there is no reason to believe that these repetitions would have to be entirely slavish and *verbatim* copies of the original. They might fluctuate in point of detail, just as two physical behaviour-processes manifesting the same habit (for example, two occasions of shaving) need not exactly resemble each other. It is even easier to imagine the occurrence of garbled versions of the original, containing useless excrescences and blurring the implicit logical connexions, and not unlike the recitations of an imperfectly learnt passage of verse. This sort of account would often suffice to describe small talk, polite essays, political discussion, and works of supposed learning.

A great deal of the use of language, therefore, may be ascribed to the working of habit. It may well be true that an account in these terms is incomplete, but some of the objections brought against it are unjustified. One of these is that in making behaviour automatic or reflex, the account makes it " mechanical " or " unconscious " : that to describe any mental or verbal process in such terms implies that the agent is really unaware of what he is doing. This is a confusion which results from using " unconscious " in two senses. Certain reflex actions, such as digestion, salivation, and the beating of the heart, are unconscious in the sense that we are never or rarely even aware of their occurrence ; others, such as the knee-jerk reflex or blinking the eyelids if something is waved before the eyes, are unconscious, or " performed unconsciously " in the quite different sense that they are not normally planned, and cannot normally be inhibited. But we can be perfectly well aware that these reflex movements are occurring, and normally have both visual and kinaesthetic sensations as constituents of this awareness. Similarly, we may not consciously plan some verbal or non-verbal activity prompted entirely by the force of habit, but can nevertheless be fully conscious that we are performing it.

This misapprehension has arisen because the account of behaviour in terms of habit has sometimes been unnecessarily doctrinaire. Psychologists like Watson seem not to experience vivid mental imagery, at least of the visual kind, and seem also to believe that to study such data experimentally is unprofitable. But to have asserted on these grounds that imagery, and other mental or introspectible experiences, do not occur at all, is an excess of zeal. Perhaps it was inspired by hostility to the traditional method of describing such experiences by reference to a thinking substance or Ego; but if so, the hostility went too far. A primitive meteorologist who denied that storms depended on angry storm-gods, might gain followers; but if he were to add that because there were no angry gods, there were also no storms, but only beaten-down crops, he would find his influence decline.

There is another criticism sometimes made of any attempt to explain even some occasions of using language as outlined above. One can offer such an explanation, it is said, only if one has failed to see that the difference between a sign and a symbol is fundamental. The latter cannot have evolved from the former. This can be seen from their properties. Signs and symbols may both have meaning, but only symbols can be used to form complexes having truth or falsehood. Signs conform only to scientific *laws*, symbols are subject to *rules* prescribing how they should be used, not how they are used. A sign means some other particular event, but the meaning of a symbol is essentially general.

Sign and symbol, then, though similar in some respects, are different in kind. Because this is so, the employment of the latter in thought and language cannot be evolved from responsiveness to the former. There must be a *saltus naturae*, an innate idea of symbolization must come to fruition. Until this happens, *language* is not being used at all. Miss Langer [1] appears to hold this opinion. She quotes the following passage from Helen Keller's autobiography,[2] and implies that Miss Keller's experience typifies a perhaps unnoticed internal revolution in everyone's mental history:

> As the cool stream gushed over my hand she spelled into the other the word water, first slowly, then rapidly. I stood still, my whole attention fixed upon the motion of her fingers. Suddenly I felt a misty consciousness of something forgotten — a thrill of returning thought; and somehow the mystery of language was revealed to me. I knew then that w–a–t–e–r meant the wonderful cool something that was flowing over my hand . . . I saw everything with the strange, new sight that had come to me.

The same criticism can be formulated by asking " How do we derive the idea of ' idea ' ? " — that to which Croce refers in the phrase " the non-empirical concept of ' concept ' ".[3] A spoken or written word is nothing but a noise or a mark on paper ; and such it would always remain, did we not interpret it as significant by virtue of an understanding of significance which we do not derive from language, but bring to it.

This objection is based on an erroneous notion of what it means to say that a sentence is true or false, or that a word is a symbol or is part of a language. Expressions like " true ", " false ", " a symbol ", " part of a language ", and so on, are treated as if they had implications like " shrill ",

[1] *Op. cit.*

[2] *The Story of My Life* (1936 Edition, pp. 23-24). When two years old, Helen Keller was deprived of sight, smell, and hearing through illness. Later she was taught to use and understand a touch-language, and then to read, write, and speak.

[3] *Logic* (D. Ainslie's translation, 1917), p. 50.

" long ", " a palindrome ", or " part of a pattern ". This supposition is mistaken. A word is a symbol, a sentence true or false, not by virtue of any intrinsic property, or relation to other objects, but because they do or would stand in certain quite elaborate relations to one or more persons. One might put the point controversially by saying that a language becomes a language not when it acquires speakers, but when it acquires students; where the most rudimentary form of student is one who does not treat certain expressions as misleading signs (like deceptively dark clouds), but classifies them explicitly, and says " that is *false* ". Similarly word-noises become words when they are classified, discussed, or legislated for by students of the language, whether professional or not.

Strangely enough, this conclusion is proved by closer examination of one of the very points introduced in raising the difficulty. Had it appeared that word-noises obeyed laws, but of some quite novel kind, it might have been necessary to suggest that they possessed unique intrinsic qualities. In fact, however, the empirical generalizations stating how and when word-noises occur are very similar to those about any other form of animate behaviour. What is entirely different in form is the language rule; but this is not discovered, it is prescribed. This prescription establishes (actually in a somewhat ambiguous way) that henceforth certain marks or noises will stand in the elaborate relations mentioned above to those prescribing the rule. A complex word-noise is the utterance of an indicative sentence, if there is someone who will say that it is true or false; and a single word-noise really becomes a word, if someone asserts that for him it is a symbol or is part of a language (which means that he prescribes rules for its use).

The confused criticism which we have been examining assumes that every user must, as it were, also be his own student; and that further, he must be in some way thinking of his words in the manner of a student whenever he speaks. The same technique must be employed (perhaps also in a cursory and telescoped manner) by anyone understanding the utterances. By this means the actual word-noises themselves become, one might say, gilded; or they are invested with an aura which surrounds them and makes them more than noise. Miss Langer, as we saw, at least speaks of " the quality of *meaning* " in posing her problem, even though subsequently she rejects the expression. This is to slip into thinking of " a symbolic quality " as if it were like " a shrill quality ". But as we saw above, an examination of the words " true ", " false ", " symbol ", etc., shows that they imply nothing about how either speaker or hearer classifies the sounds uttered, or whether they spoke in a routine way, or intelligently. They imply only that the utterances would be classified in a certain manner by some person or persons not specified — in short, students of the language. Nor can it be said that although the speaker is perhaps ignorant of any words like " true ", " meaning ", " symbol ", and the rest, he is nevertheless operating with the corresponding ideas. All empirical evidence shows that in learning these words we do not find ourselves given a name for some notion we possessed all the time. Learning to use " symbol " or " sentence " is very like learning to use " texture " or " timbre ". It is learning the former words which makes us view utterances in a new light ; just as learning the latter causes us to see familiar things in a new detail, with a new interest, and as having aspects hitherto unnoticed by us. Moreover, the conclusions of Chapter II operate here with double force. If awareness of the universal *doghood* fails on analysis to account for the intelligent use of the word " dog ", then *symbolhood*, in the mind of someone who does not know the word " symbol ", is the ghost of a ghost, and its virtue in explanation is fictitious twice over.

The objection which has been examined is not therefore

valid. A man from whose vocabulary such words as "true", or " false ", or " symbol " are absent is not obliged to utter other word-noises only in the manner of a parrot. He can interpret speech or writing as he interprets frowns, smiles, laughter, or furtive unease, and use language in the same way that he frowns, smiles, laughs, bows, steers a car, dances, or climbs a rock-face.   None of these activities is necessarily wooden, reflex, or stupid.   What can make them intelligent must now be examined.

CHAPTER IV

DOES INTELLIGENCE EXIST?

IN the last chapter the use of language was reviewed as a normal part of human behaviour, different only in detail from any other activity. Moreover, this behaviour was itself thought of as consisting of conditioned responses to various stimuli. The life of the individual was a life of habit: his conduct following a predictable, unenterprising course, his environment determining his behaviour, rather as a chameleon's colour is determined by his background. Though not asleep, though not somehow inanimate after all, these were his limits.

What behaviour, if any, does this account omit? In order to resolve this question, attention must be focussed on that stage at which a habit or response to stimulus is not yet settled, but is still embryonic. It is clear that when a well-established habitual response exists, there is little prospect of behaviour not governed by habit. The region of uncertainty is where habits are not yet formed; where the individual is faced with experience of a novel kind, and is obliged to solve a problem for the first time.

It is worth while to consider Watson's attempt [1] to explain initial successes in terms only of habits and chance. Although his views are no longer widely held, at least in their original form, they are instructive because their deficiencies are clear; and these result in large part from Watson's belief that " success " need not be referred to in describing how behaviour develops.

[1] J. B. Watson, *Behaviourism*.

He examines, for example, how an infant tries to open a box of sweets. The box can in fact be opened only by pressing a certain button. Performing this action, which we will call A, is one of the many possible things that the infant may do to the box. Watson argues that he does A with less and less delay, and progressively fewer intervening and fruitless moves, because it must occur every time that the box is opened. Therefore, of all the possible acts, A is " the one most frequently repeated ".[1]

This argument is clearly fallacious. The act A cannot occur more than once on each of the child's attempts, because as soon as it does occur the attempt is over and successful. Any other act, though, can occur an indefinite number of times on each attempt. In principle, therefore, many acts can be far more frequently repeated than A. This arithmetical approach to the problem will not do. We need to be able to say, even, that the more frequently an act has been tried, the less likely it is to recur if unsuccessful.

Watson tries an alternative argument by saying that the occurrence of A at the successful termination of one attempt increases the probability that it will occur at an earlier stage in the next attempt. But this is solely because being the last stage in an attempt involves being successful. The last *unsuccessful* acts are those least likely to recur. Discussion of the formation of habits cannot avoid reference to the consequences of actions, and whether or not they brought success.[2]

It must therefore still be asked how the initial successes which determine habit formation are obtained. Watson's view is that they are obtained by chance. The baby, opening the box, played or fumbled with it in an aimless way until it chanced to find the button and then chanced to find the sweets. He considers also a child being shown

[1] *Op. cit.* p. 206.
[2] Cf. W. McDougall, *Outline of Psychology* (1923), p. 191.

his feeding-bottle, and offers a similar account of how this is occured. He refers to the slight movements of the infant's body and arms, and points out (though without comment) that these are more and more pronounced each day. Finally, he says " the chance of the arms and the hands striking or touching the bottle before the rest of the body is great ".[1] Köhler describes how a chicken shown food through a wire screen will flutter aimlessly against the screen for an indefinite period, and only go round it if these flutterings chance to bring it opposite the open space at the end.[2] Similarly, it might be argued, of a rat attempting to escape from a maze, or cats trying to unfasten puzzle locks on the doors of their cages.[3]

These last, at least, are the sort of successes which one might wish to attribute to chance. What is involved in doing so ? One must prove the statement that a certain event happened from chance, by reference to the class of such events ; just as one must refer to the class of similar events in proving that a given event resulted not from chance but from a known cause. Asserting that an event occurred by chance asserts that there was no causally determining factor, just as the converse statement asserts that there was ; and the presence or absence of a causal factor can be proved only by reference to the class of events of the given kind. Watson's position is, then, that the class of so-called " initial successes " is a sub-class of the class of randomly determined events as a whole — a class which includes falling dice, game-of-chance machines, blind-folded persons sticking pins into maps, or roulette wheels. Living things, on this view, behave at first like dead things, but are responsive to lucky accidents.

This belief does not appear to have been tested experimentally, but in certain cases it can be formulated with

[1] *Op. cit.* p. 201.
[2] W. Köhler, *The Mentality of Apes* (1925).
[3] E. L. Thorndike, *Animal Intelligence* (1911), pp. 29 *et seq.*, p. 85.

enough precision to make experimental testing possible. Thus it might be said that rats put into a given maze for the first time get out (on the average) as fast as a ball agitated to roll about the maze at an average speed the same as the (average) rat's. The locks manipulated by Thorndike's cats might have been subjected to random fumblings from a mechanical device, and so might the box of sweets which the child tried to open.

It is noticeable that in all the above cases the problems were exceedingly difficult to solve. After all, Socrates might get out of a maze no more quickly than a rat, or even a travelling billiard-ball. If the problems are easier, are initial successes still always " by chance " ?

This is a factual question, and it may be answered from a factual source : Köhler's record of experiments with chimpanzees at the Anthropoid Station in Teneriffe during the years 1913–17.[1] There is a slight element of uncertainty in these experiments, in that some of the apes' apparently initial solutions to problems may have resulted from habits formed before capture. But this possibility is remote, and does not affect the general conclusion.

Animals of several species were shown food through a wire screen, which was so shaped that the food was obtainable only by a detour. In contrast to the chickens,[2] a dog and the chimpanzees appeared first to survey the situation, and then to take the roundabout route swiftly and smoothly, in one integrated movement. Apes jumped, without hesitation, to a position high up on the bars of their cage, the one place from which they could catch a swinging basket of fruit. Fruit lying outside the cage and beyond reach would be drawn in at once by a string attached to it.

At a later stage in the tests the apes used sticks to reach otherwise unobtainable fruit outside the bars. They did so only after unavailing attempts to use their limbs ;

---

[1] See *The Mentality of Apes, passim.*   [2] See above, p. 61.

but when the stick was brought into play, it was placed unhesitatingly beyond the fruit and used to draw this towards the cage in one movement. Then the fruit was put in an obstacle so that it could be obtained only by being first pushed away, then drawn towards the cage. But the apes, after a false start with the old straightforward method, sharply and suddenly went over to a new one; pushing the fruit from them steadily and smoothly, and then pulling it in.

The apes also learnt to use boxes for fruit hung out of reach. " The objective was nailed to the roof [of the cage] in a corner, about two and a half metres distant from the box. All six apes vainly endeavoured to reach their objective by leaping up from the ground. Sultan soon relinquished this attempt, paced restlessly up and down, suddenly stood still in front of the box, seized it, tipped it hastily straight towards the objective, but began to climb upon it at a (horizontal) distance of half a metre, and springing upward with all his force, tore down the banana. About five minutes had escaped since the fastening of the fruit; from the momentary pause before the box to the first bite into the banana, only a few seconds elapsed, a perfectly continuous action after the first hesitation. Up to that instant none of the animals had taken any notice of the box; they were far too intent on the objective; none of the other five took any part in carrying the box; Sultan performed this feat single-handed in a few seconds." [1]

Sultan, perhaps the most gifted ape at Köhler's station, learnt to make a longer stick from two short bamboos. This he did by fitting the thinner stick into the hollow core of the thicker. Idly and by chance, fumbling with the two useless sticks while the fruit lay beyond reach outside, he happened to hold them both in the same straight line. Then there came, after a moment's pause,

[1] *Op. cit.* pp. 40-41.

the sudden decisive movement to join them. Köhler's account suggests very strongly that if the first of these was an accidental movement, the second was decidedly not. The overt contrast was striking and indisputable. On being given three sticks, the ape made no attempt to join the two longer ones, but, after a pause, and in the same sudden way, fitted one long stick at each end of the short thinner one, and proceeded to draw in the fruit.

There was usually, Köhler records, this contrast between the initial and subsequent behaviour of the animals. At first their conduct is aimless and fumbling; they become apathetic or give way to lamentations or blind fury. Then after a pause comes the " genuine solution ", smooth, unfaltering, and purposeful in style. Initial successes reached in this way soon become habitual; and these can even be manifested later on in inappropriate circumstances. Some of the apes, having learned to fetch boxes for fruit hung high up, and out of reach, began by fetching them to deal with fruit outside the bars.

From these experiments it is clear that habits can be acquired in a way distinctively different from the initial success by chance. The growth of habits through chance success, through fumbling, can be cut short. In the case of the apes, this seemed to happen after some perception which was more complex than usual; not focussed exclusively on the desired object, but embracing several objects as related parts of a whole, where actions which affected some parts would indirectly affect others. Köhler, of course, would maintain that perception is often or always of such *Gestalten*. This sort of activity produces not only new habits but also makes us abandon old ones. But in these circumstances the old habit is abandoned in a way quite different from gradually lapsing through failure ; it is suddenly, decisively discarded.

There is just such a contrast between two types of initial solution in human behaviour. A man might tie a successful knot, simply fumbling with the ropes, or guess the answer to a riddle, by blurting out whatever came into his head. But the knot may also be tied, or the riddle guessed, as a result of what will for the moment simply be referred to as *insight*, or *intelligence*.

No attempt has been made to assimilate successes of the first sort to inanimate random events, in an empirically valid manner; much less has any method been suggested of assimilating the second sort. Watson suggests, at least by his examples, that it is only the first success of all — the earliest achievement of babyhood — which is " chance " in this way. Every subsequent success is facilitated by an adjoining habit. But this does no more than combine an unverified and perhaps uninvestigated assertion about early childhood, with the attribution of a power and versatility to habits which they could not possess as he defined them.

A rat's first escape from a maze might perhaps be paralleled with a certain inanimate event, in the empirically testable way required by Watson's theory. But to attempt to do this for the successes of Köhler's apes, or for intelligent human behaviour, is hopeless. Indeed, Watson should be thought of, not as attempting to put forward such an empirical theory, but as attempting to lessen the prestige of certain activities by borrowing for their description terms normally used of others.

It is interesting to notice that in the past other psychologists have fallen into an error just the converse of Watson's. He suggests that insight or intelligence is a myth; they, that unintelligence is a myth. This is true, for example, of McDougall or Watson. McDougall [1] mentions a crayfish which gradually formed the habit of taking the unblocked channel in a water tank to its food, and avoiding a channel that had been blocked. This, he says, is " intelligence at its lowest level ". Hobhouse says similarly: " When we find an animal . . . first acting in

[1] *Op. cit.* p. 187.

one way, and then, after experience of results, acting in another, we must ascribe the change to the effect of its experience. The modified action is not hereditary; it arises in and out of the experience of the animal, and indicates that in some degree the animal can correlate its own past experiences with its subsequent action. In this correlation we have already found the generic essence of intelligence." [1]

It seems that neither Watson, nor McDougall, nor Hobhouse, is advancing an empirical theory which asserts that certain facts are not what they were supposed to be, or have been misinterpreted in the sense that false empirical predictions have been made from them. Each is suggesting a different usage for describing facts, the occurrence of which none of them would dispute. This is an interpretation of Watson's view which he would not have admitted. But as he did not give his account an empirical interpretation, it is by no means uncharitable. Moreover, he was presumably aware of a difference between, for example, guessing right first time in the one way, and in the other; but did not find this an argument against his theory.

The existence of this difference, though, argues fairly conclusively against Watson's usage. For if we adopt his terminology we temporarily lose the chance to make a normal and useful distinction — that, for example, between how dogs behave, and how chickens behave, when they see food through a wire screen, or between tying a new knot by luck and by a stroke of genius. We may know little or nothing of the hidden determining conditions of either intelligent or random solutions. But we require a vocabulary for drawing attention to the one and to the other, and the terms " by chance " and " through insight " provide it for us.

Indeed, phrases like " by chance ", " by luck ", " accidentally ", and the rest, apply to human behaviour

[1] *Mind in Evolution* (1901), p. 82.

in a manner which has sometimes been quite misunderstood. In using them we do not in the least wish to argue an analogy between the behaviour of which we speak and that of inanimate objects. We have no idea of such a parallel, or of how we could set about showing that it exists. We employ the expressions for the purpose not of analogy, but of contrast. They enable us to distinguish one kind of animate behaviour from a sharply different kind. " Chance success " has meaning because it stands counter to " intelligent success ". Deny that the latter has meaning, and all the meaning left to the former is a lingering overtone of scant respect, the ghost of a distinction that has been obliterated.

CHAPTER V

HOW INTELLIGENT ACTS ORIGINATE

W E conclude that routine and chance do not account for all the behaviour of either animals or humans. There is also intelligent behaviour; and as soon as this is established, it is natural to ask what accounts for that. What makes behaviour intelligent? What occurs, between the starting-point and the brilliant jest or the idea of genius, which determines the sequence to be so strikingly different from the triteness of small-talk or routine? What, in fact, causes intelligence to be manifested?

A brief survey of what causal explanations are like is a necessary preliminary to this enquiry; and it will be a survey of how causal explanations occur in common speech, not in exact science. This is for two reasons. First, certain philosophical theories are to be criticized, and they are not formulated in the language of science. Second, it is desirable to clarify the meaning of several types of expression, used in common speech to account for intelligent behaviour, but dangerous because they encourage false philosophical theories.

By the non-scientific use of the word " cause " is meant its use by carpenters, mechanics, schoolmasters, or general practitioners, in contrast, let us say, to its use by physicists. A scientist conducting a laboratory experiment seeks to formulate laws which describe continuous processes of change (at least to the level of quantum physics). Normally, he claims that between any two observations separated by a temporal or spatial gap, a third observation can be obtained.   There is rarely any practical difficulty in obtaining this intermediate observation ; if it cannot be done with the measuring instruments in use at the time, they can be replaced by others which are more sensitive. This illustrates an important feature of scientific experi- ment.   The initial conditions relevant to the observations can usually be modified with slight and approximately equal difficulty.

Non-scientific causal enquiry is different in important respects.   First, there is spatial and temporal discontinuity between cause and effect, because observation of the inter- mediate stages is beyond the plain man's resources.   For him, causes and effects are those snatches of the scientist's continuous processes which he himself can observe without equipment or training.   Moreover, he can easily change some of the relevant initial conditions, but others he cannot change at all.   In ordinary life, environment can be modified only at certain crucial points.   But practical causal enquiry is conducted for the purpose less of abstract classification and increased knowledge than of control ; and so these crucial points become in fact the object of enquiry.   This is what makes important the distinction between what will be called here " initiating events " and " standing conditions ".   This distinction is well known. It can be illustrated by referring to a gas-lamp fitted with a pilot jet.   The initiating event which has as its effect the shining of the gas-light is turning on the gas-tap ; but for practical control there are various standing conditions, such as the presence of a supply of gas, of an atmosphere, an ignited pilot jet, intact pipes, and so on.   For the plain man " the cause " of the light is turning on the tap, because this is what he can do to bring it about.

Sometimes, however, it is desirable or necessary to vary the situation by control of the standing conditions. This arises chiefly where one wishes to prevent occurrences rather than bring them about. The gas company interested in economy is concerned to know that the existence of a supply of gas is a standing condition for the efficacy of turning on household taps. The shattering of windows in an air raid is prevented by replacing brittle by splinter-proof glass. Enquiry into both initiating events and standing conditions is relevant to practical control, though the former, for the most part, more immediately.

Distinguishing sufficient and necessary conditions is of relevance to this non-scientific type of causal enquiry. In a strict terminology the initiating event is neither a sufficient nor a necessary condition of the event which it is said to cause. But in a simpler enquiry the standing conditions are often taken for granted. Then the question "Why did the event (the shining of the light) occur?" will be an enquiry for an initiating event (turning on the tap) which, in the given context, will be a sufficient additional condition. If it were not sufficient, it would be inadequate for control. It will usually not be a necessary condition, because from the practical standpoint events may be caused in more than one way. Enquiry about the standing conditions, on the other hand, will usually be for a necessary condition, of such a kind that withdrawing it will prevent the occurrence in question.

How are initiating events or standing conditions discovered? In every case this must be done by observing a number of sequences of the given kind. The techniques for analysing the class of these sequences are well known. It should, however, be noted that in the type of causal enquiry now under consideration, the observed regularities need not be without occasional exceptions. That they preponderate is sufficient.

Scientific enquiry and everyday enquiry differ in another important respect: the sort of regularity which constitutes an explanation in the two types of enquiry. No scientist is satisfied with a causal explanation of a particular event which says only that all observed states of affairs, in the given initial conditions, develop in the given way; far less, that this is true of most such states. This point is in fact reached, sooner or later, in any explanation, however rigorous or informed. But any scientist would say that when it was reached, his power to give explanations had ceased. He would not claim to account for a given event unless he could refer it to structural details in the participating objects, which were observable independently of the sequence of events in question, and by reference to which it could be shown that the particular regularity was a special case of a wider regularity or system of regularities, systematically associated with the observable structural details.

For example, a chemist, asked to explain a certain reaction of a given speed, might point out that one substance involved was a member of a certain family of different substances, and that their behaviour in these conditions could be systematically correlated with their chemical and physical properties in general. On further questioning he might refer these regularities to their molecular structure, and these in turn to the atomic structure of their constituents, and finally to the electronic structure of the relevant atoms. In each case, an explanation is a reference to some wider system of observed regularities. It is never sufficient to say only that situations of this type always develop in this way. Scientists would not claim that this reached the level of explanation at all.

In everyday life, however, explanation of this sort is permitted; and it is permitted because it is useful. The purpose of such enquiry is the control of environment, and to know what regularly happens is a valuable contribution to this programme. Thus many words in common use can be employed in explanation, although they assert only isolated regularities. In given cases it might be asked, " Why did that glass break when dropped ? " or " Why

did the gas burn when that tap was turned ? " To answer
"because glass is brittle ", or " because gas is inflammable ",
is useful, because these generalizations serve as guides to
action. By their aid one knows what to avoid, and what
to insist on, in the future. These dispositional qualities
are very frequently referred to in explanation of everyday
events. They can, incidentally, admit of exceptions in
individual cases. Glass, though brittle, does not always
break ; gas, though inflammable, is not always ignited by
flame ; and so on.

To summarize these conclusions : " explanation " has
more than one sense, and even non-scientific causal
explanations can take more than one form. They may
function by reference to an initiating event, or by reference
to standing conditions. In either case it is legitimate to
speak of a " cause ", although the distinction between a
sufficient and a necessary condition is not made. As in
more rigorous explanation, evidence must be taken by
observing regularities in classes of sequences of events.
But to say of a particular event that it happened because,
in the given circumstances, an event of that kind always
happens, may be satisfactory from the non-scientific and
practical points of view, although it is not in a more
rigorous enquiry.

With these considerations in mind, the problem of what
causes intelligent behaviour can be resumed. Suppose that
the question " What is the cause of an intelligent action ? "
is interpreted in the first sense. It then means " What is
the initiating event which (given certain standing conditions) is a sufficient condition of the intelligent action in
question ? " For example, given certain standing conditions of interest, being awake, being in a good state of
health, not being gagged, and many others perhaps, what
is the initiating event of a brilliant jest or subtle and
original plan or gifted chess-move or masterly stroke in
playing cricket ?

The usual supposition is that such a question is perfectly straightforward. But difficulties arise when we try to define the class of events to which reference should be made in seeking an answer. Normally, in explaining some physical event, or a habitual response to a stimulus, the class may be defined by reference to the standing conditions and the initiating event itself (though still, as such, in question). Then every member of this class is also characterized by the effect event. But with an intelligent result this is not so. An intelligent result is a deviation from the normal pattern. It does not occur wherever certain initial conditions are set up. One cannot predict that it will recur if the same conditions are tried again, or with a new agent. If intelligence is being manifested, subsequent results can be different. The next time that the initial conditions are given, the reaction may be relatively stupid. This may be because a new and yet more intelligent reaction is in process of appearing, or it may not. There may be a return to an unintelligent habit. In fact, to say that an intelligent result has occurred usually implies that the normal regularity, observable in a habitual response to a stimulus, has disappeared. Either the circumstances are such that to them there is no habitual response, or there was once such a response but it has been abandoned.

It is not a simple matter, therefore, to explain what causes intelligent action in any given situation, and this for two reasons. First, the intelligent action, so far from instantiating a known regularity, is normally intelligent precisely because it departs from one. Second, there is an indefinite variety of intelligent solutions to most problems. Nevertheless, if there is to be a causal explanation of the normal kind, a regularity in the sequence of events must somehow be discovered ; and the usual method is to seek it in a new place. All the time, it is claimed, there is an initiating event which (or some variety of which) is common to all the sequences culminating in intelligent acts, and absent from all those not so culminating. But it is not an external event like hanging up a basket of fruit or posing a riddle. This additional and crucial initiating event is psychological, is some activity of the agent's mind. This may set it beyond our observation, but not beyond his; and certainly does not make it unreal.

Here at last, then, is the kind of event which causes intelligent action; and now, knowing what is relevant, we may infer from cause to effect, or from effect to cause, just as it suits us. Thus an intelligent sequence of overt behaviour, whether performed in words by lips or pen, or of some other kind, such as the steps of a ballerina, is explained by reference to prior performance of certain mental activities. The behaviour was not routine or stupid, it is claimed, because the agent " used his head ", he thought about it. Intelligent verbalization is explained by acts of prior acquaintance with the meanings of the terms used. The converse argument is occasionally advanced by philosophers : provided we perform mental acts of a certain kind, our thinking is necessarily logical and intelligent. That it ever ceases to be so is *ipso facto* proof that we have momentarily failed to perform them. We have simply ceased to think; while we are really thinking, we cannot fall into error or commit stupidities.

These accounts contain certain latent contradictions. For of any mental event which is referred to as the distinctive initiating event in an intelligent behaviour process, and consequently as the cause of the intelligence displayed in that process, it may be asked, " Is this distinctive mental event itself intelligent or not intelligent ? " If it is not intelligent, there is no reason either to suppose that it is a sufficient condition of intelligent results, or to deny that it can occur as a constituent of behaviour processes in which intelligence is not manifested. But if it *is* intelligent, then, though it may perhaps serve to explain any later intelligent behaviour, the original problem is not solved, but merely transferred to an earlier stage in the whole sequence of events For since we have assumed, in opening the enquiry, that the fact that an event manifests intelligence may be explained, it may now at once be asked, " Why is this mental event, explaining subsequent intelligence, itself intelligent ? " If an answer is given to this question, by reference to a still earlier event, then the problem is immediately transferred once more.

This difficulty cannot be overcome by the aid of a conclusion noticed above, that intelligence is not either wholly present or wholly absent, but is manifested in varying degrees. For the question which exposed the imagined explanation of intelligence should really be formulated, " Does the distinctive mental event manifest some degree of intelligence, or no degree of intelligence ? " Nor can a way of evasion be found in the time-honoured device of asserting that it is after all improper to give either a positive or a negative answer, since the question itself is improper. If those psychological initiating events which differentiate intelligent from unintelligent behaviour sequences are themselves neither the one nor the other ; and if no explanation can be vouchsafed of the paradoxical decision that intelligence-predicates are inapplicable to a certain class of psychological events, intimately connected with events admitted to be intelligent, then we create more puzzles than we solve. The original purpose was to explain an element of intelligence, by showing what caused it ; but to say that an intelligent event is caused by a prior psychological event of which one may predicate neither intelligence nor its converse is no explanation, because it is incomprehensible.

The result of this investigation is thus a dilemma : if the event referred to as explaining the intelligent element in the sequel is itself not intelligent, it cannot serve as an explanation, for it could occur equally well in a sequence which was devoid of intelligence throughout; if, on the contrary, the event referred to in the explanation is itself intelligent, then intelligence has already arrived, and the source of its arrival awaits investigation at an earlier stage.

These difficulties have arisen because we have attempted to push the enquiry beyond a point at which it would normally be dropped. A plain man would say that the event which initiated the intelligent culmination was the external event itself, which could be common to intelligent and routine solutions, or sequences not involving a solution at all. The answer to " What made him utter that brilliant retort ? " or " What made him execute that subtle chess-move ? " would refer only to his hearing what a companion said, or observing his opponent's move. The intelligent sequel would be traced, not to a prior event, but, perhaps, to a difference in the standing conditions. This aspect of the problem will need further discussion below.

The attempt to locate a stage in the behaviour process which accounts for the intelligence of a subsequent stage must be abandoned. This has important consequences. It implies that at whatever stage intelligence first appears, its appearance is inexplicable in terms of a prior stage, about which the problem of initial appearance does not arise. Consequently it is only a contingent fact, if a fact at all, that intelligent activities of one type occur only subsequent to intelligent activities of another.

This fact has been overlooked in a way which it is important to recognize. It has been supposed that there were certain mental activities which could and indeed necessarily did result in intelligent behaviour ; but about these activities the question of the genesis of intelligence did not arise. In particular, thinking could in one way or another be intelligent without a problem arising ; but overt bodily activity could not. The problem that arose as to how overt behaviour became intelligent was solved by referring it to prior mental activity. Such mental activity might take the form of thinking in words or in images of any other kind ; but for the picture to be complete, it had ultimately to be validated in its turn by reference to those incorrigible mental entities, " meanings " and " concepts ". The intelligent climber thought out his moves and holds beforehand ; the boxer fought intelligently, because he could think intelligently about boxing. Overt behaviour without prior thought was necessarily " instinctive ", " automatic ", " routine ", " reflex ", " thoughtless ", " stupid ", and the rest. Indeed, this has an initial plausibility ; " If a boxer is not thinking what he is doing," it might be said, " is he not boxing *wildly* ? How could he possibly box cleverly, unless he gave his mind to it, and *knew* what he was doing ? "

This view is now exposed. If we persist in supposing that the emergence of intelligence is explained by reference to a prior event, then its emergence at any stage is equally a puzzle and equally inexplicable. Consequently there is no reason to suppose that its emergence in overt and bodily activity is more puzzling than its emergence in mental activity. If it were found that bodily activity was intelligent only derivatively, only when it issued from a prior stratum of mental cogitations and decisions, then this would be a contingent and indeed surprising fact. Indeed, there is very good reason to believe that this is not the case ; that intelligent overt behaviour on the part of ballerinas, sailormen, mountaineers, carpenters, cricketers, and many others, is frequently quite spontaneous. In these fields it is possible to " think " (in the sense of " solve intelligently ") with one's hands, or one's feet, or one's whole body. A singer giving an intelligent rendering of a piece of music at sight frequently thinks with his larynx, and is thereby one of the few illustrations of the views of the Watsonians.

Sometimes, indeed, the attempt to think out each step in an operation beforehand, in order to perform it well, is a form of over-conscientiousness which inhibits a flair for acting intelligently in a spontaneous manner. This is frequently true of after-dinner speakers.

In certain cases, admittedly, the practical problem of intelligent and skilful bodily activity can be simplified, if some associated intellectual problem can be solved first by thinking, and this solution then be applied in the practical field. This transference, however, is useful chiefly to performers of a certain type; it is useful chiefly to those who are less than fully adept in the practical activity, and are relatively more skilful in performing intellectual operations. Thus the novice boxer is told to " think what he is doing ", but if the veteran boxer begins to do so, his fighting slows down. This fighting, however, is not " routine " ; its problems are not soluble by routine, because no two opponents give identical performances throughout a fight. Even among novices, not all are advised to " think what they are doing ". We advise the struggling and not very successful beginner to keep the maxims taught him continuously in mind ; but the promising beginner is advised instead to be bold, to " forget what you've been taught, go in and fight ". Thinking it out as one goes along is a roundabout but less strenuous method which may help the second-best. This is not confined to making use of rules and maxims governing an activity. The tyro-mountaineer or public speaker may try to keep, in thought, one or two moves ahead of where he is in fact ; and in doing so reflect on both maxims, and particular holds or phrases. His performance will be uninspired, but he may save himself from catastrophe. As he improves he can gradually dispense with this cramping safeguard.

Another point must now be considered. What is involved in the process whereby the intelligent performance of one activity, such as thinking out a solution in advance, causes or makes possible the intelligent performance of another, the practical implementation of the first ? Here too there are complexities, which were glossed over in the

references to " solving the problem at an earlier stage ".
The adequate implementation of thought in action cannot
be a matter of routine In the first place, however small
the gap between the mental planning and the subsequent
overt implementation, there is a definite time interval
during which something may occur to render the first
plan obsolete ; and although a fresh plan to stop and plan
again may be formed, it is in fact true that adjusting execu-
tion in these circumstances is commonly a spontaneous
piece of intelligent extemporization.   In the second place,
planning of this kind is usually only done in outline ; and
the details are settled spontaneously as the case proceeds.
But these details may be settled in an intelligent or unintelligent manner.   Last, even if the planning stage is
entirely specific, and implementation need only be a copy
of imagination in reality, nevertheless this copying process
cannot be executed as a pure routine.

This assertion should perhaps be amplified.   Habitual
conditioning may produce responses which are not perfectly constant, because the process is not defined precisely.
Thus the knee-jerk reflex may be more or less rapid and
more or less intense.   But a response which involves the
precise matching or copying of some previous determinant,
whether constituted by external objects, images, or anything
else, necessarily involves more than automatic routine.
There can be a routine to do one thing at a given stimulus,
and indeed to do it within certain general limits of fluctua-
tion.   But always to execute something which bears a
constant and an appropriate relation to anything with
which one is confronted, whatever it may be, requires concentration and finesse.   One may, in a reflex way, be
amiable on meeting a new acquaintance ; this involves no
intelligence and can become automatic ; but to match his
style and degree of amiability exactly by one's own cannot
be automatic.   Similarly, there can be simple routines to
act in a particular way on a given stimulus, and this

stimulus may perhaps be a mental one. But the ability to suit the action to the thought, whatever this latter may be, will necessarily involve intelligence; just as it would be involved in copying, or caricaturing, the movements of another person, whatever those movements were.

At an earlier stage two types of causal enquiry were mentioned : that for initiating events, and that for standing conditions. In order to acquire a terminology adequate to describe the more flexible and adaptable capacity of implementing mental plans, this second type of enquiry must be considered. Do any standing conditions, prerequisites of intelligent action, help to explain it as a scientific enquiry can explain a change in the culminating event of a causal sequence, by referring to a change in the initial circumstances ?

The answer appears to be that standing conditions of intelligence can be traced, and are of two types : relatively unimportant conditions approximating to those found in scientific enquiry, and more important conditions differing from them in important respects. The first type is concerned with health, nourishment, absence of mental or physical strain or fatigue, and so on. The presence of these conditions, or the degree to which they are present, can in all cases be investigated quite independently of intelligent or unintelligent performances. There is as little need to refer to displays of intelligence in testing the conditions, as there is for a chemist to fragmentate a piece of glass in order to show that its molecular structure explains why it broke on a given occasion. The psychological conditions can also be checked indirectly. That an individual is anxious or fatigued can be shown by reference to his own statements, or to his reflex responses, and does not necessarily involve reference to how intelligently he is behaving, or does in general behave.

These conditions do not usually explain why one person behaves intelligently and another does not. But they may explain variations in the degree of intelligence which a given individual displays at various times. " He has been dull all day," we say, " why is he so bright now ? " It is a satisfactory answer to say that he was tired, but has just been sleeping, or was hungry, and has just had a meal, or was anxious, and that this anxiety has been removed. These statements constitute explanations of the change, because intelligent performances are regularly correlated, in our experience, with the physiological and psychological condition of the performer.   Deviation from a certain loosely defined optimum condition makes intelligent behaviour progressively less likely because more difficult.

Favourable conditions of this kind are neither necessary nor sufficient for intelligent behaviour.   They do no more than increase the probability that it will occur, if the external initiating events are propitious ; rather as reducing the speed or steadying the movement of a target increases the probability that a marksman will hit it.   The correlation, moreover, is probably much lower and less regular than similar correlations in random mechanical processes. Fatigue and the other unfavourable conditions affect some individuals far more than others, and the same individual to different degrees at different times.

But these conditions will not explain why one person solved a particular problem more intelligently than another, or solves a problem in one field more intelligently than a problem in another.   In the everyday field of non-scientific enquiry, however, there are methods of answering such questions, and they are frequently employed.   They involve the use of words like " shrewd ", " tactful ", " witty ", " dexterous ", " musical ", " artistic ", " humorous ", " sure-footed ", " judicious ", " sensible ", " resourceful ", " charming ", " kindly ", " eloquent ", " lucid ", " deft ", " agile ", " persuasive ", " reticent ", " affable ", " gentle ", and many others.   Some of these words are ambiguous and have uses other than their use in explana-

G

tion of individual intelligent performances. But between them all there is a clear affinity. What part do they play in explanation ?

Explanations can utilize these, rather as non-scientific explanations can utilize words like " brittle ", " inflammable ", or " elastic ". The explanation says nothing more than that a particular problem was solved deftly, for example, by a given agent, because this agent normally achieves deft solutions in circumstances which offer scope for them. One frequently hears requests for such explanations in ordinary conversation, introduced by such phrases as, " How did he succeed in . . . ? ", " How did he manage to . . . ? ", " Why . . . ? ", where these enquiries refer not to the motives, but to the abilities of the agent. To such a question as " Why did he sort out the logical issues so well, and then explain them so offensively ? " it might be proper to answer, " Because he's very clear-headed, but not a bit tactful ".

Words in this class refer to and collate the responses of an individual, but these responses are by no means of a constant kind. Saying that a climber is agile, or that a diplomat is discreet, or a conversationalist witty, does not mean that their agility, discretion, or wit is always manifested by the same overt performances. Indeed, this would be impossible. What is agile in one situation would be fumbling, useless, or reckless in another ; what is discreet on one occasion is insulting on another ; remarks which are sometimes witty would be out of place at other times. The expressions mean that, throughout a whole range of varying problems, the agent can be relied upon to vary and modify his reaction, so that on each occasion it is appropriate, but each time in a new way. An agile climber climbs each pitch differently, and if he failed to do so would not be agile.

In consequence, the explanation of an intelligent solution is given by drawing attention, not to an unvarying

or virtually unvarying response, but to a capacity for flexibility and adaptation, which will have a new device in
store for each fresh trick that circumstance may play.
The words under discussion refer to " talents ", " accomplishments ", or " skills ". Not all of these are at the same
level of generality ; some are relatively specific, and others
more general abilities which can be manifested in a number
of different directions.   In this more general class are
words like " versatile ", " astute ", " sharp ", and " intelligent " ; the most general term of all is perhaps " clever ".
It can be observed empirically that ability to produce
intelligent solutions in one field of activity is usually
correlated with similar ability in certain others ; and this
fact receives vague and fragmentary recognition in the
loose and indeterminate hierarchy of ability-predicates in
ordinary language.

One of the tasks of empirical psychology is to investigate these correlations by precise and scientific methods ;
and the invention of intelligence-tests is the invention of
intelligently soluble problems, which satisfy the following
requirements : successful solution is correlated to a high
degree with successful solution of problems in general,
and the degree of success can be easily calculated and
expressed in a quantitative manner.   It is unnecessary to
assert that those correlations which are found are determined by a family of faculties thought of as entities constituting the furniture of the mind ; the only way in which
these faculties can be further investigated is by studying
the very behaviour which they were introduced to explain.
Consequently what is offered is not a scientific, but a
pseudo-explanation. This methodological principle, however, is more recognized now by psychologists than it was,
and need not be laboured.[1]

A particular intelligent act, as was established above,

[1] Contrast Spearman, *The Nature of Intelligence*, pp. 12 and 26, with
C. Burt, *The Factors of the Mind*, p. 218.

cannot have its intelligence explained by reference to a distinctive prior event. But it can be explained in the manner of the second type of causal enquiry, by referring to a regularity in the behaviour of the agent, and pointing out that the given act is no more than an instance of it. This regularity, however, is not of the specific type resorted to in non-scientific explanations of particular physical events, but of the flexible and generic type which constitutes an accomplishment or skill.

Thus, although a certain type of causal explanation cannot be given for the intelligence manifested in intelligent actions, it is not true that no explanation is possible; and, indeed, words of the class that have been examined are significant because they can enter into explanations of this second type. Furthermore, it is still possible, in principle, that a third and scientific type of explanation could be given. For should our knowledge ever be such that behaviour can be exhaustively correlated with physiological conditions, then the deviation of an intelligent action from the established response pattern might be precisely explained. This explanation would perhaps take the form of correlating particular varieties of intelligent solution, not with prior initiating events, but with distinctive differences in the initial standing conditions. But more precisely, the distinction between event and condition would itself probably become artificial, as it does frequently in scientific investigation; for intelligent re-action could, at this stage of knowledge, be studied as a complex of continuously changing processes, and its study would be a part of normal science.[1] Whether such explanation will ever be possible in fact, however, is quite an open question.

We can now consider how mental or verbal plans are implemented in overt action; for plans are implemented by virtue of some of those accomplishments or skills

[1] Cf. C. Burt, *The Factors of the Mind*, p. 216.

which are used to account for particular intelligent acts. Implementation is a generic ability, involving not doing the same thing over and over again, but doing anything, whatever it may be, which executes the plan in question; and just as other higher-order dispositional qualities are referred to in a special vocabulary, so this talent is sometimes what is meant by " practical ability ", " efficiency ", " executive ability ", or " organizing ability ". Success in implementation varies with the conditions facilitating intelligent action, just as the other talents do. Adverse physiological or psychological circumstances may not at first reduce the ability of a dancer or climber to imagine intelligent solutions, but will nevertheless be likely to render the implementation of those plans clumsy, unintegrated, or slipshod. Conversely, it is when these conditions are most favourable that practice tends most to improve upon theory.

Considering how intelligence is manifested in giving effect to plans emphasizes once again that acts can only be intelligent if they serve a purpose. It is of no importance whether the purpose is consciously thought out, as sometimes with human beings, or exists only in the sense that a fox after the chickens has a purpose. There must be something which the agent is trying to do. This is what makes it possible to distinguish between the generic intelligence- or skill-predicates, and physical predicates like " brittle ". At first sight there seems to be a difficulty, for properties of this latter kind exhibit fairly wide variation. Two pieces of glass, given exactly the same blow, rarely fragmentate in the same way. But this flexibility does not tempt one to attribute intelligence to the glass; there is no characteristic pattern of adaptation to environmental changes, in relation to a relatively fixed system of trying to achieve certain results. Should that appear, the glass would be called " bewitched " ; and the connexion with intelligence is clear.

The general problems of intelligent behaviour have been considered in order to obtain a fuller understanding of what is involved in the intelligent use of language. It is time to return to this more special problem. But it will be remembered that the scope of the enquiry was originally widened, by discussing not intelligent activity, but habitual response; and problems of language must be postponed for a chapter, while something is said of the interrelations between intelligence and habit.

CHAPTER VI

HABIT AND INTELLIGENCE

BY now it is established that, in describing the behaviour of organisms, intelligence cannot be left out of account; and further, that certain accounts of its genesis are misleading. There are two other ways, however, in which we may attempt to give an account of intelligence : by comparing it with habit, and by considering not the cause, but the signs of its presence.

There are two senses of the word " habit "; and corresponding to them are two senses of " intelligent ". Much confusion has resulted from not noticing this, and contrasting, in consequence, the unrelated uses of the two words; so that it is important to make this distinction clear. First there is the sense of " habit " in which to say that a man has a certain habit means that his behaviour is in this respect inflexible, machine-like, and unrelated to his needs. For example, he has a habit of reading the paper at breakfast. He does so every morning without fail. It makes no difference that he has ceased to enjoy reading it, or that, either regularly or on a given occasion, he inconveniences himself by doing so; read it he does, with the regularity of clockwork. If there is no paper, he becomes moody and restless, and cannot eat his breakfast properly. This is " blind habit ".

But there are habits of quite a different kind, which we refer to when we say " he has a habit of going to furniture sales ", or " he has a habit of judging men by their actions, not their words ", or " the Chairman habitu-

ally sums up the discussion in a brief concluding speech ",
or " he has a habit of saying things that are much wiser
than you think at first ". We should deny that, in this
sense, a habit even could be " blind ".

For each of these senses, there is a sense of "intelligent ".
In one sense of this word, that an action was done intelligently directly implies that it was not done from habit, and
conversely. Intelligence means what it does because it is
a contrast with habit, which refers to stupid routine.
Here there is no smooth gradation from unintelligent to
intelligent, but a sharp break. Actions, and people too,
indeed, are either intelligent or they are not. The other
sense of " intelligent " is that which emphatically provides
for a gradation from the less intelligent to the more. This
time, every action, and every person, has some degree
of intelligence, and might always have been better, or
might have been worse. Imagine a schoolmaster to say,
" I have only seven intelligent boys in my class ; the most
stupid boy is no more intelligent than a rabbit ". Here
he uses the word first in one sense, then in the other.
The distinction may also be traced between those habits
into which we say we have fallen, and those which we simply
acquire.

The two senses of " habit " may be said to correspond
to the two senses of " intelligence ", because we should
tend to deny that actions manifesting habits of the blind
sort showed any intelligence at all, and to claim that an
occasion on which such a habit was decisively thrown off
was a definite sign of intelligence, pure and simple. But
on the other hand, habits of the second type (such as
making speeches which sum up discussions) show themselves in actions which manifest intelligence to a greater
or lesser degree, but which can scarcely be quite devoid
of it. This therefore is intelligence in the second sense.
Besides this, there is another factor which relates the two
pairs of senses. Living organisms are presented with

problems which tend toward two quite different norms. First there are those like having to give a speech, or encourage someone who is known to be depressed, for example ; these may be done with any degree of success, but can scarcely be not done at all. If we call them intelligent, we naturally tend to use the second sense ; and there seems no place here for the first sense of habit. Second, however, there are problems like getting a banana into a cage by pushing instead of pulling, or solving a cipher, where the obvious distinction is between complete success and complete failure, and where it is difficult to see that of two successful solutions one could be the better. These situations lend themselves rather to the first sense of " intelligent ". At the same time they lend themselves only to the first sense of habit ; for if we miss the successful solution we either do nothing at all, because nonplussed, or else persevere blindly in accordance with a habit in this sense, pulling vainly at the fruit, or applying the routine technique, without avail, to the cipher.

There are thus these two senses of " habit " and of " intelligence ", and in the first of them (though not the second) they are mutually exclusive terms. Now a purely contingent fact has brought it about that these various senses have been confused in a most unfortunate way. The contingent fact is that scientists, studying the formation and development of habits among animals under laboratory conditions, naturally tended (and properly within limits) to study the easiest cases first ; and there were cases where an almost unvarying stimulus produced (if anything at all) an almost unvarying response. Even when they restricted their problems less stringently than this, they tended to consider stimuli, and responses, which varied only in a simple, quantitative manner. But necessarily, habits of this kind are almost always ideal instances of blind, slavish habits. The other sort of habit by no means lends itself to laboratory examination. What resulted from this trend ? Since " habit " was used in the first of its two senses, " intelligent " tended to be so used as well, when the two were spoken of together. But when these are the senses adopted, an action which manifests a habit, by that fact alone, does not manifest intelligence. Scientists have thus often been willing not to quarrel with the philosophers' claim that intelligent action springs from a different source ; and it has been easily possible to argue that the tendencies of habit formation and growth are unrelated to the solution of new problems by intelligence or insight. These confusions have encouraged philosophers to reject the scientist's account in the case of intelligent actions, and push forward with a special account of its genesis invented by themselves. This account has already been discussed.

The scientist's account, though, does not refer only to habits in the first sense of the word. It refers also to habits in the second. In this second sense, habits are as much as ever dispositions to responses which can be inhibited or conditioned. If one has a habit of judging Englishmen by their actions and not their words, one will tend to do so with Frenchmen, or Chinese, for example. Yet these habits not only are not manifested in an undeviating or slavish manner ; they cannot be. Each time the situation is likely to be novel ; not in all respects, but in some, almost certainly in more than one. It offers, perhaps, an analogy with the past, but the analogy is only partial. Each time, also, the response which that situation calls forth will be different. Suppose, for example, that a man has the habit of crossing fords by the stepping-stones. In each river the stones are differently placed, and so must be his footsteps. Something in the nature of insolence evokes something in the nature of a snub ; grief evokes solicitude in one way or another ; and a rabbit somewhere in the garden will elicit a corresponding stalking performance from the cat.

There is, as we saw, no reason why a manifestation of one of these flexible, responsive habit-dispositions should be not intelligent; but more than this, almost every such manifestation must be more or less intelligent in our second sense of that word. The very variability of the responsiveness means that the situation may be well or ill responded to; and the better it is handled, the higher the degree of intelligence that the action displays. The best solutions, since they show a high degree of intelligence, will of course also be intelligent in the first sense.

But before these claims are substantiated, it must be shown how such actions really can be based on a habit, and yet intelligent too. This can easily be done by reverting, in the first place, to the instance of a man with a rigid habit of reading the paper at breakfast. His actions display no intelligence because, however the situation varies, his response will not vary. There is no adjustment of one to the other, because one does not change at all. On the other hand, a hostess who, by habit, welcomes each arriving guest, but is reserved with the hearty ones, familiar with the dignified, and patronizing to those who are conceited, offends every one; and her conduct likewise displays no intelligence. Her responses fluctuated, perhaps wildly; but there was no intelligence, because no adaptation to the changing case. Conduct of the first kind tends towards stupidity, that of the second towards silliness.

Had this hostess wished to avoid giving any more parties, though, her behaviour might have displayed intelligence to a high degree; and this brings out the important point that what constitutes the successful solution depends upon the desires and purposes of the agent. But if these are given, it is then possible to make a general statement about the likely results of intelligent action. It is that in situations presenting only an incomplete analogy with the past, behaviour is adapted in just the ways and to just the degree which will secure that even in the new case the old requirements are satisfied. As the intelligence of the organism increases, its improvisations on the basis of its past can be more profuse and ambitious, its jumps into the partly unknown more daring, the adaptation of its behaviour to the novel case more refined and delicate. The past is never wasted, and never abandoned. But if a part of our environment offered no analogy, however remote, with any prior experience, it could only leave us bewildered; and any behaviour entirely without parallel in our own history could never be intelligent, it could only be unintelligible.

This adjustment and adaptation to the novel, perhaps the wildly novel, is what is likely to occur when an organism is behaving intelligently. Something can also be said of the conditions of awareness which promote such conduct. The organism must be aware not only of one or two obvious features of his environment (such as the clock, and the newspaper), but of the whole of it, notably its less conspicuous though perhaps more significant features. Then he may manifest intelligence in either of two ways: he may extend and adapt the play of a habit on the basis of a slight and obscure analogy with the past, or may refrain from behaving in a well-practised manner (despite a clear and powerful analogy), because he is sensitive, this time, to the warning of some partial and obscure difference. This is the contrast between invention, creativeness, originality; and critical insight, or ability to correct errors.

Something must now be said of the prolonged or continuous sequences of action, in which several different habitual responses are integrated; as, for example, when a soldier unlimbers a gun, a musician performs a much-rehearsed concerto, or a speaker at last delivers his long-prepared speech. Here two false suppositions may arise, and although they seem to be opposite in tendency, they really spring from the same cause.

The first is, that even if the previous discussion has successfully shown that isolated intelligent acts may not be breaks with the whole habit-equipment, but developments of it, nevertheless the integration of responses must be a different kind of process. Combining routines is more than a routine operation; perhaps it must be even planned or thought out, certainly it is intelligent in a sense not yet discussed. This belief, however, attempts to rigidify the distinction between a single response and a continuous sequence of responses, whereas this distinction is quite arbitrary. It is arbitrary, because no action is so brief and simple that it has no constituents. Even responses like pointing, or picking something up, or uttering a single word, are really complexes of many different movements, and this is overlooked only because combining them has now become completely routine. Conversely, almost any behaviour-sequence, however long and involved, could under suitable conditioning be initiated by a single primary stimulus. Soldiers are trained first to perform one by one the constituent actions of unlimbering a gun, and then to combine them all into a single routine sequence evoked by a single word of command. It is unimportant whether the subsidiary stimuli, evoking further responses within the series, are the soldiers' sensations of the gun itself, progressively unlimbered, or of their own completed actions. These latter, as with a gymnast or dancer, might suffice alone.

Moreover, even elaborate sequences of actions are not necessarily intelligent. They may be either intelligent or slavish, and it is easy to see that the distinction suggested above in respect of the single action applies equally to the sequence. Unintelligent soldiers, once drilled, will go through their complex routines blindly and slavishly, cling to the fixed routine even if circumstances are novel, and run into errors which are noticed, if at all, only after they occur. But the intelligent soldier limbering up a gun on the edge of a cliff introduces exactly the requisite degree of deliberation into his movements, although deliberation was by no means provided for in his training; if he knows there is a great hurry, omits just the incidentals which, this time, can be dispensed with; if he is preparing for a long journey, limbers up his gun with an appropriately special thoroughness. In every case he omits, includes, modifies actions as that case requires. Deviations from the standard pattern may be trivial or significant; but (remembering the two senses of " intelligent ") *if* they are intelligent they conform to the requirements of the given case, and they *are* intelligent to the degree to which they conform.

So much for the first of these two false suppositions. Now for its apparent converse : this is to argue that although the intelligence manifested in a sequence may involve only a refined adaptation of established skills to a partly new case, solving an anagram, or seeing that two things will fit together, and so on, requires something more. On this view the prolonged sequence of behaviour is what least displays the distinctive character of intelligence; what most displays it is the isolated, indivisible problem. Here the subject completely succeeds or completely fails. He does not have simply to modify a well-known technique, but is in an impasse from which he can only escape by, as it were, a leap.

This point is really a reversion to one already discussed. It is enough to recall the distinction between situations which can be solved well or ill, and those which can be solved or not solved. The isolated indivisible problem may be of the second kind, and this may encourage the use of " intelligent " in one of its senses; but this does not prevent its use elsewhere in the same sense, and should not cause us to forget that it has another sense. Moreover, it must perhaps be emphasized again that situations not requiring a " leap " may also not be soluble merely by trivial or unadventurous adjustments in learned routines. The extemporization may have to be brilliantly original here too ; the climber, the dancer, the public speaker, given unfamiliar situations, take their life in their hands in a literal sense or otherwise, although doubtless an analogue for each of their actions is easily traceable in their past activities. But, besides this, problems offering as alternatives only complete success or complete failure can perfectly well occur in a situation dealt with by a sequence of behaviour, or even constitute the whole of it.

Both these difficulties, therefore, arise from the same confusion : the erroneous belief that a rigid distinction can be made between a single action and an integrated sequence of actions. Since both are resolved by emphasizing that there is no rigid distinction, this is a convenient place to point out in particular that intelligence is not confined either to sequences or to isolated actions which involve the use of *symbols* ; or constitute thinking in contrast to doing. What is true of an action thought of as single is true of an action thought of as a sequence. Elaborate sequences may often require a prior planning stage ; but they often do not. Intelligence displayed in a symbol-using planning sequence sometimes enables us to reduce the sequence of actions to a sequence of routines ; but, short or prolonged, swift or leisurely, sequences of actions may be intelligent intrinsically. The sequence of thinking in symbols is simply a variety and not the master-key.

So far, this chapter has suggested two main conclusions. First, that " habit " and " intelligence " do not refer to fundamentally different types of behaviour, but to different aspects of behaviour within the same range. Intelligent action tends to modify existing habits to suit every requirement of the given case. Second, when an organism is behaving intelligently it is aware of the significant but unobtrusive elements in its environment ; and performs a modified version of an established act, because of a tenuous similarity, or refrains from the normal action because of an obscure but warning difference.

But although, if behaviour is intelligent, these statements may be true of it, still they do not enable us to distinguish intelligent behaviour from unintelligent. The first does not do so, partly because if the situation is not novel in any respect, the most intelligent and the entirely routine solutions coincide; and they must be distinguished, if at all, on other grounds. Besides this, it offers little or no help in respect of actions which in fact are classified as " intelligent mistakes ". The second does not provide an adequate criterion, because it is exactly a question at issue whether, so far from using awareness of obscure analogies or differences as a criterion of intelligent action, we should not have to use the intelligence of the action as our clue to the awareness.

There are, however, several senses of the word intelligent which we have not yet distinguished. They fall not parallel to, but athwart the two forms of use distinguished above; but only one of them is relevant to this discussion, and two others must be noticed so that they may be set aside. First, it appears that " intelligent " may perhaps be used to refer only to the relation between an act and the situation in which it occurs, without reference to the agent. In this sense, the intelligence of an act appears to be in proportion to the elaborateness of the problem it attempts to solve, and to the degree to which it approximates to the ideal solution, as that is determined by the desires and the environment of the agent. Intelligence is to be estimated from the laws governing whatever makes up that environment, and from their number and complexity; it is, as it were, a simple product of complexity and aptness. The second sense of " intelligent " is in question when we ask how much credit the agent deserves for his solution, and refer for an answer to how his past experience could have aided and guided him. The criterion of intelligence makes reference here to the established corpus of his talents ; and we rank his performance higher as we believe that he was obliged to extemporize. But this problem arises for us only if we decide already that the performance was intelligent in a third sense : that it did not result from chance, and that (though it might indeed not differ from acts which he has done before, and could perform by routine) it was in fact not the product of a routine habit blindly applied. This is the sense of " intelligent " which concerns the present discussion, because it is the sense which underlies such expressions as " he had his wits about him ", " he was alive to what was going on ", and so forth ; and because of this it is often argued that in this sense intelligent action is essentially and completely dependent upon the occurrence of certain distinctive mental events. Thus, apparently, what we have already discarded as the cause of intelligence, insinuates itself as its criterion.

What, then, are the criteria of intelligence in the third sense ? Two general types of answer tend to be given. The first is that our guide to its presence in a given action is that the agent can show that this particular success does not stand alone, but is merely one instance of his general competence to solve a wide range of problems of this kind, novel or otherwise. We present him with cognate difficulties, ask him to improve on what he has done already, or comment upon it, or elicit its principles, or train other people, or describe different ways of failing to solve the problem, or whatever else it may be. In brief, the criterion of intelligence refers only to the performance abilities of the agent.

The alternative account claims that this only touches the fringe of the problem. The real proof that behaviour was intelligent is that it was done with understanding or insight ; and to know this we must know something of the state of mind of the agent. Did he act thinkingly, did he really

H

know what he was doing? Was insight present? If the word " mental " is used to mean " in the mind " or " not perceptible by others ", like mental images, for example, and unlike mental arithmetic (where there may be no introspectible intermediary between hearing the problem and giving the answer), then this account of intelligence claims that the criterion of intelligence is whether or not certain mental events occurred.

Now if it is urged that these events are signs of intelligence because they are its causes, then the account reverts to a view rejected in the previous chapter. It is necessary here only to say that what is being sought at present is an empirical criterion of intelligence, and that a criterion of this kind would not be empirical. It comes from a theory that intelligent action can only be initiated by thinking; and the presence of the mental events initiating it is inferred from the action itself on these theoretical and *a priori* grounds, not only without the support of evidence from introspection, but often in apparent defiance of it. Though, since the theory is not empirical, it would be impossible to confirm or refute it by evidence.

But this account may take another, less controversial form. It may not refer to mental events which bring intelligent behaviour about, but only to certain mental data which accompany and indeed are a part of that behaviour. The occurrence of these mental data is the criterion of intelligence, but not its cause. Such an account will perhaps be developed as follows. There is an easily recognizable difference, it might be said, between what it feels like to do an action mechanically, automatically, or, as we say, " unthinkingly ", or (perhaps under orders) without understanding its full significance; and what it feels like to do the same action with insight and intelligently. This is true, in different ways, first of doing something straightforward, like copying a document, which can be done blindly or intelligently; and second, of crucial actions which solve isolated problems either by insight or by luck. An essential part of making a joke or solving an anagram is that the agent *sees* the joke, or sees that his solution really is a solution. Being bewildered is feeling bewildered ; understanding is feeling that you understand. It is not easy to describe these introspectible differences, and usually it is done in metaphors : " it was all as clear as daylight " ; " I saw it in a flash " ; " the light dawned " ; " I was quite stuck ", and so on. But that they are difficult to describe does not alter the fact that they are familiar to everyone, and are the criteria of intelligence.

The distinction is all the clearer, it might be added, if we think not of actions, but simply of watching or following something. There is all the difference in the world between how it feels to see an event happen, and be aware of its significance, and how it feels to see the event and be unaware ; or between reading a sentence and seeing its meaning, and reading it but being none the wiser. Subsequent performances may be closely related to this understanding, but do not constitute it. That we understood something at one moment might bring it about that we could behave successfully later, but does not mean that we should do so. If we are successful, it is success in a related but separate field ; and conversely, if we fail, it is a separate failure. Successful performance is thus neither a necessary nor a sufficient condition of understanding. Indeed, understanding, which does not involve any action of our body, makes especially clear that mental activity, and notably active thinking itself, is intelligent not because it can be supplemented, but because of its feel ; because, to use metaphor again, we are illuminated and we have insight in executing it.

From this it is but a short step back to almost the first form of the account : to the claim that for intelligent thinking the occurrence of the symbol-sequence is neither necessary nor sufficient. The real criterion is the glow, or the flash, or the daylight atmosphere of genuine insight; and those states of mind of which we say " I know the answer, but I can't just put it into words ", are naturally quoted as confirming this argument.

Thus of these two accounts of the criteria of intelligence, one says that the criteria make mention of an agent's abilities in related fields of action, the other that they make mention of distinctive introspectible states. Before any attempt to choose between them, certain objections to each must be examined. First, in respect of the introspective criterion, it must be admitted that the alleged psychological differences between the understanding and the blind act are sometimes difficult to trace. It might be very hard for an actor, say, to identify just the psychological element which was present when he uttered a speech in a play, understanding its meaning, and absent when he uttered the same speech without following it at all; and yet it is alleged that this is the element which shows the first to be a comprehending, and the second a rote activity. Sometimes, of course, it would be easy to identify this differing element; but to provide an adequate criterion, it must be possible always. Moreover, while this sort of criterion lends itself to one sense of " intelligent ", it does not do so at all to that sense which admits of a continuous scale of degrees. Again, it can only be applied indirectly to persons other than oneself, and this raises special difficulties, and suggests that for this psychological criterion to be sometimes applicable, it must also sometimes be superfluous. For in order for us to know, by this criterion, that another person's action was performed intelligently or understandingly and not by chance or as an automatism, he must first observe his own psychological condition, and then describe it to us. We must be sure, moreover, that both these activities were intelligently performed, especially the first, which easily admits of error; for if we are not sure, the evidence that the primary activity is intelligent is inconclusive. But we

cannot be made sure by further introspecting and description on his part; for if the intelligence of his introspecting
and describing activities is in question, evidence given by
them is inconclusive. Sooner or later we must allow that
at least some of his behaviour is intelligent on other grounds,
and if we do this, we abandon the psychological criterion.

Even, then, if the psychological criterion is sometimes
utilizable or even decisive, apparently it must sooner or
later be supplemented. But one may doubt if, when it is
useful, it provides either a sufficient or a necessary criterion
of the presence of intelligence. It is not a sufficient condition, because it is often deceptive. A solution to a
problem dawns with all the glow of authenticity; but
ultimately it proves to be no solution at all. We read a
sentence with every psychological sign of understanding,
and then find that we have understood little or nothing.
We even recognize certain conditions, such as fatigue or
strong prejudice, in which it is more likely than not that
such a criterion will mislead.

Nor is it a necessary condition. First, there is no
particular and distinctive glow of insight, or daylight
quality of understanding, which is requisite for any
particular action or sequence to be intelligent. At the best,
it is any flash or flood of intellectual light, of whatever
particular psychological quality, which will do; and in
consequence this criterion is very much vaguer than it
seemed. But second, and more important, there is no
need to assure oneself that these mental data have been
part of a person's experience, in order to decide that he
has acted intelligently. Even were we sure that they had
not been included in it, we could pronounce the behaviour
intelligent. There may easily be persons whose behaviour
has for themselves a psychological character totally different
from any with which we are acquainted; or which has
no psychological character whatever. Yet other evidence
could assure us that it was intelligent.

Would this other evidence be, as was suggested by the first account of the criterion of intelligence, that the agent could display other abilities related to his ability to solve the given problem ?   One is tempted to argue that this is so ; but there is an objection to this account parallel to one objection urged above against its rival.   Suppose it is said that a given action's being intelligent, and not done by blind routine or chance, is established when it is established that the agent can solve cognate problems, or improve on his first performance, or train others, and the rest.   Must not these auxiliary performances, to suggest anything about the intelligence of the first, be themselves intelligent ? Just as, on the psychological criterion, the intelligence of behaviour can be established only through intelligent introspection, so here, it seems, can it be established only through intelligent supplementation.   This could be put another way : if all that the agent has is a disposition to solve cognate problems, his intelligence is unproven ; for a disposition may be simply a blind habitual tendency. What he must have is a genuine ability or capacity to do so. These words would not be used unless it were clear that the manifestations of the tendency are intelligent manifestations ; and whether he really has a capacity, or only has a disposition, may very well be a question.

But there is a reply to this objection : one which follows a well-known philosophical pattern.   According to the account under examination, the intelligence of an action A is to be confirmed by showing that in certain conditions other actions, say B, C, and D . . ., will occur.   If the intelligence of these is challenged, it must be established according to the same technique by proving that others again will occur in appropriate conditions, and so on indefinitely.   But the intelligence of act B is established by establishing the occurrence of other actions, including C and D, and also including A.   The evidence for the intelligence of further acts referred to in due course (say E, F, G) is in part the occurrence of B, C, D, and A itself. If the challenge is made again and again, one of two things happens: either, as the field widens, the later actions are failures, and in this case the evidence, according to the performance criterion, is negative; or else if they are successes consistently, it becomes more and more difficult to know where to look for the sort of evidence which would suggest that the first stratum of evidence was misleading. The evidence for the later evidence consists more and more of the earlier; and that, by hypothesis, was favourable.

But, it might be said, does not this reduce the whole argument to a circle? In a sense it does, but not in an important sense, for two reasons. First, evidence of this kind constitutes an *argumentum ad hominem*. It is normally addressed to someone who admits that such a thing as intelligent behaviour really exists, and further that certain sequences of behaviour are instances of it. He is not raising a question about the whole range of action which is covered by the steadily widening favourable evidence, and consequently it is enough for him if the behaviour about which there is controversy can be shown to be homogeneous with that about which, so far as he is concerned, there is not. The existence of capacities for success in an indefinitely wide field of different but related problems is evidence to satisfy him, because his chief concern was to exclude other hypotheses: that the given behaviour was a lucky shot in the dark, or one example of a blind routine.

The second reason why the eventual circularity of evidence of this kind is not important is that a person who raised about this whole corpus of varied success the same question as he had raised about each part of it, would still have to admit the distinction which this criterion of intelligence establishes. The distinction is simply that actions which have a semblance of intelligence prove on investigation sometimes to be entirely isolated or associated only with a blind and inflexible routine, and sometimes to be members of an indefinitely wide and varied assembly of other similar actions. If this distinction is admitted, then whether it is called a distinction between intelligence and its absence, or by some other name, is a triviality.

The two criteria of the presence of intelligence may now be compared; and it is not difficult to see that in their actual use, the psychological criterion and the performance criterion largely interact. Each may sometimes be taken independently as a direct criterion of intelligence; but much of the importance of the psychological criterion is that it is an indirect sign of intelligence, because it reliably indicates that the performance criterion would also be satisfied. Further, that the psychological criterion is normally subordinated to the other is confirmed by our rejecting it as misleading, should the psychological data and the performances give contradictory results. For example, if we persistently feel the psychological illumination of insight but find ourselves unable to exploit our understanding in respect of new problems, we admit fatigue or illness and cease to trust our intuitions. As for saying " I know the answer, but I can't put it into words ", past experience makes us confident that feelings such as we now have will be shortly followed by ability to give expression to our insight, though we cannot do this for the moment. But if it proves this time to be not so followed, we retract, and say " I suppose I didn't understand after all ".

This subordination is illustrated by another case which at first sight seems to disprove it. We sometimes give a person credit for understanding a word in a foreign language, though he is unable to translate or use it. This suggests that we believe he understands, when we believe that he has a certain mental experience from seeing or hearing the word used in a given case. But we never believe this as an article of faith. We believe it (if we do at all) because although he cannot succeed in activities like translation, which are the usual index of understanding, he succeeds in others : for example, he is able to offer a series of possible translations, and reject them for what seem to us to be convincing reasons. If he were unable to exploit his understanding in any way, we should decide that there was no substantial evidence of it.

Nor can it be argued that even if psychological evidence is of interest chiefly as a sign that the performance criterion could be satisfied, evidence about performances, in its turn, is relevant to the presence of intelligence, because it is a sign that the unique psychological condition of insight has occurred. For so far as this last expression refers to a condition whose presence or absence can be empirically verified, the discussion has established that we do not require to know the introspectible detail of another's experience in order to assert that his behaviour was intelligent; or even to know that there was anything introspectible in it at all. Yet the impression may remain that though the performance criterion may be more influential, the other is more intimate, comes nearer to the essence, as it were, of really intelligent action or genuine understanding; and the last problem of this chapter is to point out why this is so.

It is because many of the expressions used to describe the introspectible experiences associated with intelligence are also used to assert that the behaviour in question really was intelligent and not routine. " He came to understand "; " then he understood "; " he realized what was going on "; " he saw what he was doing ", are all expressions of this kind. In one of their senses they are simply synonymous with assertions that some behaviour was intelligently performed; in the other sense they are not synonymous with, but inconclusive and subordinate evidence for, these assertions (though it is perhaps because this evidence lies readiest to hand that they become synonymous). But as there is this sense in which they are synonymous, and therefore, if they are true, the assertion about intelligence is necessarily also true, it is assumed that when they are interpreted as affording empirical evidence, they still afford evidence which necessarily is conclusive. This is a confusion which has only to be pointed out for it to disappear; and yet it is this confusion of a distinct statement offering evidence, and a synonymous statement offering only a verbal tautology, which has caused this criterion of intelligence to be estimated so erroneously.

CHAPTER VII

VERBAL LANGUAGE, ITS CONTEXT
AND SUBSTITUTES

THE argument must now make its way to verbal language; but this it cannot reach in a single move. We have gained some insight into the activity of using symbols, by comparing it with other, independent forms of behaviour; now it must be compared with the forms of behaviour which accompany and supplement, or even replace it; and which contribute to the same ends as the process of using symbols itself. What these ends are, in detail, is the subject not of this chapter but of the next; here the problem is that, whatever they are, they are served not only by that single strand of behaviour which consists in using the symbols, but by many other elements in behaviour as well. These other elements are obscured if symbol-using utterances are considered only by considering written sentences which are verbatim reports of them; for such written language records almost no element in the original speaker's behaviour, except that single strand. Not written versions, but all the details of particular occasions must be examined; or we shall withdraw attention from just those aspects of the case to which, for the moment, we wish to give it.

If a verbatim report of a speech, consisting wholly of a sequence of written sentences, is contrasted with the speech itself, these further elements can easily be traced. They may be divided into two classes. First, the speaker's utterances were delivered in a certain tone of voice and with a certain verbal emphasis; and he may have accompanied them by pointing or gestures, or by changing facial expressions. Of these, although they are generally recognized as important accompaniments of, or alternatives to, using verbal symbols, the report makes no mention. But there are other elements, important too, though their importance is usually overlooked. The written report does not even specify that the utterances it records were utterances of the same speaker; nor (assuming that they were) whether he stood still while he spoke, or moved, and if so, when; nor what were the intervals of time between, or indeed within, his utterances. Yet all these questions are necessarily answered for anyone who hears the utterances, since he is presented with a complete performance, not a partial report. The experiences which give these answers are so simple and straightforward that they are often overlooked in discussions of the subject; but they may be crucial in interpreting the verbal strand itself.

The verbatim written report which has been contrasted here with the real performance would be rather unlike such a report as one might find in a newspaper. If it is to offer a complete contrast, it must contain nothing whatever but the verbal symbols employed; but such is the importance of the elements which this would ignore, that we normally incorporate, into written reports, certain typographical devices like " ! " or " ? " or " . . . ", or using italics or beginning a new line, which do not themselves represent verbal utterances as the written words do, but indicate, instead, some of these supplementary elements. Further, of course, written reports of speeches and conversations usually contain verbal comments by the recorder, comments not merely reproducing the verbal utterances, but describing any part of the original performance which the recorder thinks important. The present problem, however, is not whether some few of the additional elements can after all be recorded in written form, but what they are, and how they are important.

So far these elements of gesture, facial expression, voice-modulation, and the rest have been described only as supplementing the use of verbal symbols, though as modifying, perhaps, their significance. But this is an incomplete account. These devices may contribute independently to the ends to which using verbal symbols contributes. Pointing silently, nodding or shaking the head, shaking one's fist, shrugging one's shoulders may occur instead of words, and supplant them. Nor is there only a small number of such gestures with independent significance; the number is large, and new gestures are frequently added. Facial expressions may have independent meaning too. So may more complicated forms of behaviour like mimicry and dumbshow. Some of these devices (winking, for example), so far from merely modifying, may actually cancel and override a verbal utterance. They are not essentially subordinate; essentially they are independent of verbal utterance, and their subordination, when it occurs, is fortuitous.

The variety and importance of these non-verbal alternatives or modifications to verbal utterance is clear. Their origin must now be considered; apparently they may arise in either of two ways. Some of them, clearly, are learnt specifically as forms of behaviour which contribute to the ends to which using words contributes, in that they can modify the significance of those words, or take their places. They are learnt as language is learnt, and for the same reasons; their use is governed by conventions which may vary between one nation and another. They may even be introduced to others by verbal definitions and explanations, and be offered either by themselves or in conjunction with some verbal utterance, as identical in meaning with this or that form of words. Examples are clapping to applaud, hissing, nodding and shaking the head, or turning down one's thumb.

Between these and the other class there is no sharp line, but even so there is a clear difference. Smiling, laughing, cheering perhaps, frowning, shaking the clenched fist and stamping the foot, in their varying degrees, are independent of using language. They may originally be learnt, it is true ; and it is likely that, like language, they will if learnt at all be learnt through imitation. But these modes of behaviour, it seems, would be acquired even by a man who learnt no language, and never attempted to do what men normally do by means of language. This is easy to see. They occur readily and naturally when we are alone or unconscious of others ; they may not be universal tendencies of behaviour, but they do not vary from people to people like those discussed above ; they may be learnt, but can hardly be taught ; there are no conventions for their use, and indeed, that they are used can hardly be said at all.

If it were not for one fact, modes of behaviour of this second type would be no more intimately connected with the verbal language than blushing or crying, which as symptoms of one's condition may in a sense, after all, convey information. But there is an important difference. Blushing and crying are normally beyond control ; or at least cannot be induced, though they may be suppressed. But smiling, frowning, and the rest can be performed more or less deliberately, and this gives them, or can give them, a quite new status. They may not simply occur when and where chance decides ; they may be utilized, developed, adapted, exploited to contribute to the ends to which using symbols contributes. There is no simple contrast between their occurrence fortuitously, and by design ; the agent may introduce any or all of these modes of behaviour, with greater and greater concentration, deliberateness, and effort, as instruments of his purpose. Since, moreover, they now occur as purposive behaviour, they may be performed more or less intelligently. Thus intelligence can manifest itself, with equal ease, in using symbols or in behaviour which does not use symbols, but has the same character because it is directed to the same end.

Not everything that can be done by words can be done otherwise, admittedly. But gestures, facial expression, shrugging the shoulders, and so on, can frequently do what words would do; and, moreover, such behaviour can have, among others, the gentle, or brusque, or condescending *nuance* that would be possessed by this or that verbal version, nicely chosen for its exact significance. There are two further points. We may not simply exploit these devices of behaviour intelligently, to be a substitute for words; but they may accompany a verbal sequence, and delicately and subtly modify its import. Simple routine words with skilful supplementary behaviour may have the same effect as skilfully chosen words by themselves; this can be traced in welcoming a visitor or pointing out one object among many. Again, it is not only those modes of behaviour originally acquired independent of language that can be intelligently adapted for linguistic purposes. The other, conventional devices are not fixed and inflexible routines. Nodding and shaking the head, or clapping, for example, can be adjusted to give a *nuance* apt in the given case and perhaps in no other; and they too may have effect alone, or may complete and enrich the meaning of a verbal sequence.

So far, gesture and facial expression have received fullest consideration, but the conclusions about their origin, development, and utility largely apply to the various modulations in speed, volume, or *timbre* of the speaking voice, and to the non-verbal utterances, like gasps or sighs, with which it may be punctuated. It is more difficult than ever, in respect of these aspects of the use of language, to tell what is likely to have been acquired to function like or with language, and what, originally, independent of it.

But even so, one may easily trace the same progressively more deliberate exploitation, or progressively more intelligent adjustment and refinement. We raise our voice, speak more quickly, utter our words with greater decision or emphasis, to indicate our exact degree of eagerness or confidence, or the exact magnitude or intensity of what we speak of. We gasp at first, perhaps, quite spontaneously ; but a practised speaker may, on occasion, do so in just such a way as indicates that he is frightened, or shocked, or vexed, or surprised. By the tone of our voice we can indicate that we are in any of a variety of emotional conditions, or that we speak in jest or ironically or for form's sake. In all these instances, perhaps, the devices are as effective as language, but not through any convention, through a tendency independent of language. Even so, they can take the place of language or reinforce its point. These elements in using words are often virtually indispensable, if we are to be understood at all. It is very difficult to make oneself believed, or to be not misinterpreted, if one speaks in an inappropriate tone of voice, or uses no particular tone when one's tone would normally be distinctive.

The intimacy of connexion and the continuity between these various modes of behaviour becomes fully apparent when we recognize not only how those less specifically linguistic in nature can be developed and directed to serve the ends of language, but also, conversely, how the more conventionalized forms can retrogress so that they occur where language could not have its normal function. Conventional gestures like nodding or shaking the head may occur when we are alone ; on this or that occasion they may have a status like that natural to a blush or a sigh. They may simply be unplanned, uncontrolled symptoms of our condition. This may also happen with verbal responses. Interjections occur in dictionaries and have a verbal form, but they are not normally used to execute the

functions of verbal symbols.   Moreover, verbal utterances
themselves may retrogress from a linguistically advanced
to a more primitive function.   We talk to ourselves when
alone; or speak in company as we sigh or fidget, not to
achieve what characteristically we achieve with words; or
our tongues run away with us, as it is said, and a torrent
of words flows forth, perhaps in anger, having the appearance of intelligent speech, but being in reality something
quite different.

What is the philosophical interest of these points ?
The enquiry began by considering the nature of using
symbols, as an intelligent activity of special interest; and
what was thought distinctive of a symbol was that there
was a rule or convention endowing it with meaning and
with its characteristic status, or further, that there was a
whole system of interrelated rules performing these functions for this and many other symbols together, by trans-
forming them into a language.   But we see now that if
this is what distinguishes a symbol, then our original
interest in activities which used symbols was in part
misunderstood.   We supposed that these activities interested us because they did use symbols, whereas this was
an incidental feature; the interesting features were other
and independent.

This is so because we were interested in these activities,
as performing operations of certain sorts, and as displaying
intelligence in so doing.   It seemed as if they could perform these operations, intelligently too, because they made
use of symbols in the given sense.   Now we see that this
is not so.   The operations in question, although those for
which symbols are especially useful, can often be intelligently performed without their aid.   We have reminded
ourselves of how this can be done by movements of the
body, by facial expressions, or by non-verbal noises.
But again, when these activities are performed by using
symbols, they seldom use symbols and nothing else.   The

significance of the symbols is adjusted and qualified by other accompanying strands of behaviour, or by the precise *nuance* given them in utterance by the manner of their delivery. Nor is it true that verbal symbols are determined, qualified, or replaced only by conventionalized devices which consist, in effect, of non-verbal symbols. We draw, for performing the operations which we often use symbols to perform, upon a far wider range of human behaviour-patterns than those originally acquired for such operations. Modes of behaviour unconnected at first with the uses of any form of language are exploited and developed as we see fit, fused intimately with the characteristically symbol-using strands ; and these latter are neither essential, nor dominant, nor, always, capable of being self-supporting, nor, sometimes, even important.

Thus, though it may be the character of symbols to perform certain operations, it is not the character of those operations to be performed by symbols. But the link between the two types of behaviour that interest us — to wit, intelligently doing those things which we often do with symbols, and using symbols — is more tenuous still, for two further reasons. First, symbol-using performances may lapse, or retrogress, until they no longer serve either any of the usual functions of language, or indeed any other function. They cease to be used at all, and merely occur, no more than symptoms of the condition of him who utters them ; in respect of the operations which, frequently enough, we perform by language, the class of utterances of symbols is no more a permanent *élite*, than the class of other modes of behaviour is a class permanently depressed. Second, we may act intelligently, and have as our end one of the ends which are served by using symbols, and our action even take the form of uttering sounds which appear to be symbols ; but the reasons why our action is successful, and the grounds why it is intelligent, may still not be that the sounds we utter are symbols. Whenever we use a word in a new metaphor or extended sense, and whenever, as is sometimes the case, we speak intelligently although, perhaps because, we break a rule of usage or more precisely of what is called " logical grammar ", we infringe the system of conventions, adherence to which would be what made our symbol-like noises really symbols. If, even so, our utterance is effective or intelligent, that is not because it sounds like uttering symbols, but for some other reason.

The general scheme of relations underlying such a state of affairs appears to be this. There are three distinguishable categories : being part of a language of symbols governed by a system of conventional rules (*i.e.* being a symbol) ; being an activity which is performing one of the functions often performed by activities using symbols ; and being an intelligent activity. At one extreme is the view that the class of acts in which only symbols occur, and that of acts performing one of the functions often performed in language, are logically equivalent ; and that this class stands to that of intelligent activities, not indeed in the relation of equivalence, but in the peculiar relation that members of it cannot be members of the other, and yet must " express " such members. This view may be progressively weakened ; but the truth seems to be reached only when the three classes are thought to be logically independent. The only category about which there might be doubt is that of intelligent actions employing symbols. But given any fixed list of the functions defining the second class, it is clear that intelligent acts employing symbols may or may not perform one of these functions ; the possibility is always open, that symbols are intelligently used for a new function. When this scheme of logical relations is fully laid bare, it becomes plain that an interest in the intelligent performance of these functions prompts an interest in the use of symbols only as one aspect in several of a complex variety of activities.

It is now almost time to consider more fully these functions, often performed by language, which have been referred to with such tedious frequency, but not yet examined. Before doing so, however, we shall pursue one aspect of the present discussion in more detail. So far attention has been concentrated on cases where non-verbal forms of behaviour, or non-verbal aspects of verbal behaviour, can modify the intrinsic sense of words, or cancel or supplant them. It has been more or less assumed that the verbal strand would have some determinate significance, even if all these supplementary elements were removed. But there is a class of utterances of which this is not so. Here the verbal strand is indeterminate in a way which no verbal addition could remedy. Utterances of this kind often do, and always can, include one or more of a group of words which are confined to them, and serve, when they occur, as their distinctive mark.

Russell has discussed some of the words distinctive of such utterances under the title of " egocentric particulars " [1]; among which he includes words like " this ", " I ", " here ", " now ", and so on. But the title is not very apt, and the discussion far from satisfactory. He puts the question, whether sentences which contain egocentric particulars could be translated into others from which they are absent, and suggests that " this is red ", for example, is equivalent to " redness is part of W ", where W is the speaker's whole sense-experience from a certain place, at a certain time. But an utterance like " this is red " means much more than that. As it would normally occur, it determines exactly which part of the speaker's sense-experience has the quality of redness; and further, it somehow draws the hearer's attention to a red part of his own sense-experience. Russell tries to distinguish the meaning of " this is red " and " that is red " by saying that the first is uttered when there is a minimum time-interval between

_____

[1] See *An Inquiry into Meaning and Truth* (1940), p. 108 and Index.

the experience and the utterance, the second when there is a longer interval. Here there are two mistakes. To begin with, this is not an analysis of the difference in meaning between two expressions, but a description of the physiological conditions which respectively cause their utterance; besides this, the contrast he is discussing arises most naturally between " that *is* red " and " that *was* red ". He is examining a difference between the present tense and the past. The special function performed by " this " and " that " in contradistinction to each other is something which he fails to reach.

Russell's discussion is unsatisfactory because he attempts to discuss sentences containing these words *in vacuo*, without considering the circumstances in which they are used on this or that occasion; such a method might be successful for other classes of words, but this is exactly the class for which it is sure to be unsuccessful. Let us begin with the simplest case, " this is a penny ", for example. Here the meaning of the utterance is made determinate, because it is accompanied by a gesture of pointing, in conjunction with which it has to be interpreted. The speaker's forefinger, perhaps, forms part of the hearer's sense-experience, and a movement or distinctive position of that finger naturally draws the hearer's attention to whatever is contiguous with it; rather as a bang or a puff of smoke naturally draws attention to the figure of a marksman unnoticed before. This tendency may be more or less sharpened into a rule, until we tend to claim that someone who does not look where we are pointing is misunderstanding wilfully. As for " this " and " that ", often enough they are used indiscriminately. But their distinctive difference is that they indicate, through a convention, how the speaker's gesture is to be interpreted. For " this ", we turn attention to a region more or less contiguous to the speaker's pointing gesture; for " that ", some more distant region in a direction indicated by the gesture. However it may be, the gesture is what determines the meaning of the verbal utterance; and as we point more vaguely, or synchronize gesture and word more carelessly, the meaning becomes increasingly uncertain.

There are many different uses of " I "; only the most straightforward of them concerns this discussion, and this use is such as to make " I " and " here " to some extent analagous, as a pair, to " this " and " that ". " Here " is the more general, as it indicates the whole region of space about the speaker's body (more or less extensive according to the context); and " I " the more specific, as it indicates that physical object which is his body. The meanings of these words are not normally determined, it is true, by gestures; but nevertheless they are determined by certain conditions, less obvious than these, which were referred to early in this chapter. Sentences containing " I " and " here " have determinate meanings because the hearer can identify, as a definite part of his own experience, not a gesture of the speaker's, but his whole body; because furthermore he can tell when successive utterances come from the same speaker's body, and when they do not; because, finally, he can take for granted certain conditions such as that the spatial positions of speakers are fixed or change slowly, and that there is a negligible time-interval between speaking and being heard.

If these conditions are not satisfied, additional devices must be employed. In a large gathering, " I " and " here " lose their usefulness unless accompanied by gestures like standing up or raising one's arm. A speaker who is moving may have to accompany " here " by gestures if he wishes to make its use fully determinate.

Words like " now ", " then ", and " soon " are in part the temporal counterparts of the terms we have been discussing. Here there are important differences; but the words function rather like gestures themselves, " now " directing the hearer's attention to his experiences of the moment, " then " to memories of his past experiences, " soon " to fresh experiences as they come. Once again, the words only have determinate uses because of certain empirical conditions normally satisfied when we speak; this time, the conditions are that utterances occur at determinate times in the speaker's and the hearer's experience, and further, that they occur at the same time in both. Once again, if the conditions are not satisfied, the speaker must use special methods : should he be at a distance from the hearer, or stammer, or wish to speak of events that are very quickly over, he must supplement his verbal utterance by some gesture like waving his hand quickly, or some noise, like a pistol-shot, which performs the same function.

The words which belong to this class are not few in number, nor do they form a quaint by-way of language. This aspect of meaning can be traced very widely. In some languages it is more conspicuous than in others; what is done in English by the two words " here " and " there " is done in Welsh by three words, in Russian, I believe, by four, and in certain languages by a complicated vocabulary of the form " here to the north ", " away to the south ", and so on. But even in English, the variety of such expressions is very great. There are all the spatial expressions like " within thirty feet " or " in the neighbourhood " or " two miles off "; temporal expressions like " today ", " last year ", " five minutes ago ", and so on; words like " near " and " distant "; all personal pronouns and adjectives, which in speech may always need supplementing by gesture; and sentences like " take it away ", or " hand it over ", or " turn to the right ". All these have determinate meaning because their use in utterance is supplemented on this occasion by one part, on that by another part, of the element of actual utterance which a verbatim written report would almost entirely omit, and which embeds verbal behaviour in a significating context which is not verbal.

The question naturally arises, however, What makes it possible to use words and phrases of these kinds in the written language at all ? for the writer is usually absent, and may be unknown, so that gesture is impossible. Apparently, therefore, the conditions which give these expressions determinate significance are not satisfied. But they are satisfied in part ; though it is difficult to decide how much this results from conventions accepted by both writers and readers, and how much from features of the case whose significance is natural. Suppose, for example, that we find in a book the sentence " this is false ". That sentence has a determinate meaning through the convention that sentences in a book are to be read in a certain order ; and conventional marks of punctuation will indicate whether the sentence refers to its immediate predecessor (as is usual) or its immediate successor. A determinate meaning is obtained by setting, not the index finger, but the sentence itself, in juxtaposition with what it refers to. The case is similar when " this " is used in a sentence referring exclusively to an illustration, or when " treasure here ", with an accompanying arrow, is written in the margin of a map. Convention is less important this time, though it still establishes that these sentences are not part of the main text. Arrows and juxtaposition, part naturally, part by convention, do for these sentences what gesture and its counterparts would do for them if they were spoken. Finally, the principle is the same when a sentence like " these grounds are private " is exhibited on a notice-board. The sentence gestures for itself by being in a determinate place, and staying there.

Words like " this " and " here ", moreover, need not be used. " Litter " over a basket, " trespassers prosecuted " on a post in a wood, " no thoroughfare " by a gate, or the name of the subject of a portrait beneath it, or of the painter in the corner, all manifest this use of language in one way or another. These notices have determinate meaning, or not, depending on conditions which are very like those for utterances determined by gestures. As the gesture must successfully indicate a particular object, so the notice that says " litter " must indicate, by its position, something into which litter could reasonably be put. If there was once a basket, but it has been taken away, or if the notice is moved, the word loses its meaning. Similarly the notice can be too big for the object it designates, just as a gesture can be too broad and sweeping. Then in either case the verbal expression becomes indeterminate.

Clearly the word " egocentric " can refer only to an occasional and incidental aspect of expressions of the kinds we have been discussing; we see that the decision to examine language in a general context of behaviour is beginning to give assistance over a wide range of philosophical problems.

CHAPTER VIII

PROLIFERATIONS OF THE
VERBAL LANGUAGE

THROUGHOUT the last chapter the notion of a class of functions, not necessarily, but frequently performed by using verbal symbols, has remained before us undiscussed. What are these functions? This problem focusses attention more than ever upon the verbal language, as our typical and specially developed means of performing them. So much is this the case, that the discussion is virtually restricted to the questions, "What things may be done in the verbal language?" and "What resources does it contain for doing these things?" It transpires that these questions direct attention particularly to the use of verbal language to make statements. Philosophers have sometimes written as if this function were somehow that natural to language. But this opinion has resulted in part from an insufficiently close empirical survey of how language is used; in part from largely restricting attention to the utterances of philosophers themselves, and other educated persons; and in part from overlooking how such words as " statement " have a more or less philosophical, and a specifically grammatical sense, which are connected only loosely.

Two earlier conclusions will prove of importance in this discussion of the functions and resources of language. The first is, that uttering a word may be no more than going through a learned response on receiving a routine stimulus. The second is, that verbal responses can be evoked by just the same sorts of stimulus, and in just the same way, as non-verbal.. This second fact draws attention to the mistake made in a common assumption : it is commonly taken for granted that when a word is uttered as an unthinking response, the stimulus of the response is necessarily an object of the kind that would be referred to in a dictionary giving the meaning of the word. It may be allowed that there are exceptions, but this is the standard case : the stimuli of verbal responses are the objects they describe. " Red " will naturally be evoked by a sensation of red, " I " by an experience of myself, " approve " by a sentiment of approval, and so on. Special problems, such as how the verbal responses can be made in the absence of their appropriate objects, or how they can be purposive in other functions than describing, are then recognized by philosophers, and attempts made to answer them.

But the assumption creating these difficulties is false. There are no necessary restrictions upon the kind of object which can stimulate a particular verbal response. Everything depends upon the experience of the agent ; and this is not like the carefully regimented and stereotyped environment of the laboratory dog, but something fluid and complex, the parts of it indefinitely interconnected. The assertions of a dictionary restrict the verbal activities of no one but a man who successfully resolves to use words only for dictionary purposes and on dictionary models. Ordinary language is the language of persons unacquainted even with the idea of conforming to a dictionary. The assumption has no evidence at all in its favour. All the evidence suggests that almost any verbal expression may be evoked by any part of the speaker's external environment, or by any part of his internal sensations, bodily or other.

It was agreed that no action could be intelligent, or indeed stupid, unless it was related to some purpose of the agent. The assumption, just now rejected, about the

sort of object which would properly or normally evoke a
verbal response, was really an assumption about the purpose which employing language properly or naturally
served ; and this assumption was that the proper function
of language was to describe objects. To describe an object,
it was supposed, we uttered what was virtually the name of
that concept of which the object was an instance. " Language is given to us to express our thoughts " is another
version of the same theory. So far as thoughts are thoughts
about objects, they consist of streams of concepts which
the objects instantiate. Uttering words merely externalizes
the stream, and thereby causes the same concepts to stream
in the head of someone else.

When no arbitrary restriction is placed on the conditions
which can evoke a verbal response, it is possible to see
that the functions which verbal responses of one kind or
another perform are exceedingly various. One may go
through the actions of clenching one's fist in order to grasp
something and pull it down, or grasp and wave it in the
air ; or to frighten someone, or to hit someone, or to warm
one's fingers, or to watch how one's hand clenches, or to
practise clenching it in a certain way. Similarly a given
complex of words, or even a single word, may be uttered
for many different purposes on different occasions, each
time quite appropriately. The variety of purposes served
by language as a whole is of course much greater still ;
just as bodily movements in general serve many more
different purposes than clenching the fist.

These various functions may be hinted at, though one
cannot be exhaustive. The correct point of view is rather
that it is surprising, not if two utterances serve different
purposes, but if they serve the same. But a catalogue of
some of the functions which are served by the verbal
language will help to indicate the multifariousness of the
problem. Thus, language is used to influence the actions,
or the feelings, of the beliefs of other persons (it is scarcely

necessary to point out that to describe the true state of affairs is neither the most common nor, often, the most efficacious means of influencing beliefs). It is used, more or less recited, to influence our own feelings (war-cries serve this purpose in part), or our own beliefs (as when we try to imprint something on the memory). It is used, as in polite small-talk, to avoid awkward silences, or to conform to certain norms of etiquette. It is used to pose questions, to make promises,[1] requests, bids, surrenders, bets, and the rest (and the utterances making these things do not describe, or state that they have been made), and to count and calculate. It is used to avoid or deflect questions, either simply by taking up the time of the prospective questioner, or by confusing him. It is used to deceive, and to silence those who contradict us. It is used to enter pleas, to give testimony and make confessions (neither of which are simply descriptive), to take oath, to pray, to give thanks, and remit sins. It is used to give commands, warnings, and instructions, to make requests, and to express wishes. It is used to cause another to visualize our own states of feeling. It is used to act, to recite, to eulogize, to mourn, to curse, to compliment, to congratulate, to celebrate, to exercise magical powers upon objects, to conjure and exorcise spirits. It is used to indicate the time at which something occurs, or the time at which someone is to act in a certain manner — for example, to start races or announce their start, or to drill a squad. It is used to draw attention to gestures, or to our own location in space. It is used to remind of what is already familiar. It is used to train and educate. It is used to construct verbal complexes like poems, which conform to certain artistic requirements or canons; it is used to tell stories, and to make jokes. It is used to promulgate laws, including the rules of its own use, and to provide illustrative examples of how they

[1] Cf. J. L. Austin, " Other Minds ", *Proceedings of the Aristotelian Society*, Supp. Vol. 20 (1946), pp. 170-175.

may be kept or broken, or of any other aspect of itself. Doubtless it is used in many other ways as well.

Language is thus a practical instrument for bringing about a variety of results. But the foregoing catalogue was perhaps misleading, for it was no more than a miscellany of the functions of language. It did not distinguish between activities like composing stories or poems, which might be indulged in for their own sake, and those other uses of language employed simply as means to ends. Nor did it reveal how some of the listed functions were wide and generic, and others more limited in scope; how using language, for example, to change the feelings of another, might draw upon many more circumscribed functions like expressing wishes, sneering, reciting poetry, or uttering warnings. The catalogue may also have been confusing in another respect. There is a significant difference between, to take another instance, using language to influence others, and using it to offer a price or make a declaration of love. The latter are not alternatives to influencing, nor are they simply varieties of it; they are simplified, conventionalized devices helping us to expedite these varieties of influence. Giving an order, apologizing, mourning the dead, acting, and telling stories are also routine devices, and are introduced by, or comprise, routine formulae of speech, gesture, or posture. They are short cuts to results otherwise obtained by a more elaborate deployment of language; and if we ask why they are efficacious, we see clearly that it is because of this or that aspect of the elaborate system of known social relations within which language is normally employed.

It is worth seeing in more detail how these simplified methods are related to more general purposes. We might naturally suppose, for example, that it would take eloquence and perseverance to make someone quite convinced that we should act in a certain way. But given the English language, and also a known social context, we have only to say " I promise ". Depending upon the context, the routine takes a more or less elaborate form : the Prince's word is his bond, the soldier swears on his sword, the ordinary person must fetch a Bible, slaves perhaps cannot promise at all. If the enemy is " an officer and a gentleman ", then " I surrender " is enough ; if not, he has to persuade the victor inch by inch to believe that he has certain intentions. We learn that on appropriate occasions a certain tone of voice indicates a recitation, or certain devices of stage or costume indicate acting. When this is recognized, the verbal sequences are understood in quite a new way. The speaker can lament and we do not offer sympathy, or be insulting without our becoming angry. Children, before they can be entertained by stories, have to be taught to understand words in a new way. If we wish to understand newspapers, it is necessary to learn that news columns and obituary notices must be interpreted differently.

In English there are many linguistic devices of this kind ; and these devices are routines to obtain results which could otherwise be obtained only by special means calculated *ad hoc*. It might be said that they mechanize language. There are, for example, words like " vow ", " promise ", " undertake ", " offer ", and the rest — each, in an appropriate context of fact, affecting the speaker or more especially the audience in a definite way. There are grammatical forms like the interrogative, imperative, and subjunctive moods of verbs, which are routines for posing questions, giving commands or instructions, and expressing wishes or uttering curses. There is a special though archaic form (" would that . . .") for expressing wishes that the speaker believes are hopeless and therefore that he does not wish anyone to attempt to promote. There are a special tone of voice and special pronouns for prayer. There are special gestures or postures for pronouncing oaths and blessings. Expressions like " once upon a time " may originally have given information; now they serve purposes like those of the other devices. They are part of the ritual of language.

It is a commonplace that these different linguistic forms do not reveal fundamental modes of thought, or anything else of the sort. They are simply devices, more or less positively conventionalized and of wider or narrower acceptance, which enable persons using words to obtain the results which they use them for more efficaciously. Their general utility depends on the traditions and institutions of the society using the language in which they occur, and their utility, in particular cases, upon knowledge also of the details of the case. There is no inflexible system of these routines: most of the verbal forms themselves are largely interchangeable, and additions to their total number may constantly be made, as new types of situation are explicitly distinguished and provided for. Soldiers, for example, have developed a special use of the simple future to indicate that the order given will be regarded as having a distinctive and well-known kind of authority. Colloquial expressions like " I don't think ", " I wouldn't know ", or even " eh ? " at the end of an utterance, indicate that the speaker is being ironical, or rebuffing an unreasonable enquiry, or simply teasing, perhaps. Or again, questions in the form " Is . . . or is it not ? " constitute a distinctive brand of question, utilizable only in particular circumstances.

Strangely enough, any new routine device may create good reasons, in certain circumstances, for not using it, but reverting to an *ad hoc* method instead. This is true for several reasons. First, routine methods may be too blatant in their significance. This sometimes makes them less efficacious, sometimes less entertaining for the speaker, or his audience, or some part of his audience. A blunt warning may be ignored, a hint taken ; a plain insult may lead only to violence, a covert insult may achieve the desired results and also give more malicious pleasure to the speaker or to those who fully understand his meaning. A direct question may put the hearer on his guard, when other forms of speech would succeed in eliciting the utterances required.

But these are factors making it desirable to avoid the routine device, in order to conceal from the hearer that it would be appropriate to one's purpose. One may, however, wish actually to draw this to his notice. If the speaker is in a position to use the form of a command, and conspicuously does not do so, he might emphasize his own goodwill or friendliness. This would be a comparatively simple effect; but differences in the context or the precise tone of speaking could produce many others. Again, if the hearer is made aware of a scrupulous avoidance of the authentic formulae for, say, making a promise or a declaration of love, the effect of the utterance may be not diminished, but much increased. Or perhaps it might be pleasant to receive, in a veiled form, a request which put plainly would not be pleasant.

One further reason might induce a speaker to avoid a formula of speech, though it was readily available. So far the discussion has been worded as if it were normal for a single utterance to have a single purpose. But this is not necessary, and probably not frequent. In consequence, the formula may be rejected because it furthers one interest at the expense of another. This tendency is traceable to some extent in some of the previous examples. To illustrate it fully in a written form requires, perhaps, the powers of a novelist. For this discussion it is enough to recognize that in ordinary speech the quite unmixed motive, and consequently the quite unequivocal meaning, is comparatively rare.

There is one kind of linguistic routine and of formula serving it which has particular interest and importance. Given a certain development of experience and linguistic

K

equipment in one's hearers, one may attempt to influence and control their behaviour by using formulae which promulgate rules. In particular, one may attempt to influence and control their linguistic behaviour by promulgating rules of language; and the fact that making such rules is a distinctive activity has persuaded some people that there is a fundamental difference between using language to make rules and using it in any other way. Such a use brings us, it is thought, to a mental frontier. But rules, even when made by formulae, are not usually made for their own sake; they are made to obtain certain results, and that these may be obtained by routine methods is a contingent product of social conditions. The rule-formula is a device for mechanizing a certain type of persuading oneself or others to act in a particular manner. This is the kind of persuading in which the speaker claims that the course of action he advocates is the course which conforms to some aspect of the situation with which it is proper to conform. Attempts to persuade in this manner about using language only indicate that the speaker has recognized the making of verbal noises or marks as a distinct activity, as he might recognize dancing, or eating, or manipulating playing-cards as a distinct activity. No mental frontier is crossed when we make rules about language, except that crossed whenever we distinguish any fresh activity or object or aspect of things, and coin a word for it; or whenever we attempt to mould the behaviour of others, in any respect, by a formula instead of by *ad hoc* methods.

Persuasion does not require any special formulae when used of language, any more than when used of anything else. It is never true that language can be used in a particular way only by means of certain verbal constructions; but here as elsewhere our labours may in favourable circumstances be abridged by a routine device which makes the use explicit. Developed rule-formulae like " Let

' . . . ' = ' . . . ' Df. ", or the device of juxtaposition in dictionaries, like other formulae, crystallize a use of language of which there is a continuous ascending scale of more rudimentary forms. It is interesting to contrast the method of a dictionary, where juxtaposition, order, the use of brackets, spelling, and the rest, make it possible to promulgate rules of usage without comment, with that of a work like H. W. Fowler's *Modern English Usage*, which, because it treats of more controversial points, replaces formulae by persuasive argument.

But even so, that there are devices especially for promulgating rules of language draws attention to a significant new point. The partial catalogue of uses or functions of language given earlier obscured the distinction between using language for purposes in general, and using it for purposes which have regard only to itself. But as soon as any thing, or any aspect of it, is given separate recognition, it is possible to adopt some purpose referring to it alone. In the first instance, boats are rowed in order to propel them from place to place; but as soon as " rowing " is distinguished as an activity, one may make it one's purpose to row, to row in a certain style, to train persons to row in that style, to invent a style of rowing, and so on. Similarly, as soon as making a rule of language is recognized as a distinctive activity, one may make rules of language not for the purpose of influencing others, but only for that of making things of a certain sort; or conform to a rule not because one wishes to act in the particular way it prescribes, but because one wishes one's behaviour to be an instance of conforming to a rule of language.

But any activity, primitive or sophisticated in form, which has as its purpose to influence or control the use of language, always has the effect of recognizing that use itself (in whatever specific manner) as a distinctive kind of activity; and this recognition is of importance, because it throws light not only on several of the uses of language mentioned in the partial catalogue of uses above, but also on the relation between a large number of those uses, and the expressions " description ", " statement ", and others. This relation is important, because describing or stating are often supposed to be the typical or natural functions of language, upon which the uses mentioned in that catalogue must be superimposed.

Because combinations of words are used to obtain practical results, and because the practical results we aim at in using them are sought in an environment of objects and of persons concerned with objects, it follows that to fulfil their functions, the combinations of words that occur in utterances must, often enough, be somehow correlated with objects. These correlations exist in the form of average tendencies that run through the fluctuating and multifarious patterns of the total use of words by a social group. As the attendant circumstances change, so there tend to be changes in the combinations of words that are uttered. This reveals that there tend to be what we will call " objective " conditions for the occurrence of many verbal expressions (that is, conditions of the objects in the situation in which the expression is used). Linguistic habits, that is, are in large part determinate with respect to objects ; and the range of situations tending to be the objective condition of the occurrence of this or that combination of words (usually a sentential combination) is popularly called its meaning.

One might suppose, at first glance, that there was little likelihood that such combinations of words should often occur. If nothing prompts us to speak save the conditions of objects, it might be said, why should we speak at all ? Nevertheless, several factors make for their occurrence. We are likely to utter such combinations when, though we have some general reason to speak, such as restlessness or a desire somehow to interest our hearers, we have no more specific purpose, to be served by speaking in one way rather than another. They may also occur when the situation is unexpected and causes us to speak in surprise. Besides this, they have more serious uses. To the degree to which they are correlated with the conditions of objects, acquaintance with them can have the same sort of usefulness as acquaintance with the objects themselves. Consequently, it is often useful to formulate such combinations of words for purposes of storage. They have the same kind of utility as photographs (though of course they have a quite different kind of correlation with facts). It may also serve our purposes to make them available to others; if they correlate with situations in our experience, making them available in this way will enable others to benefit, in part, as if they had actually had our experiences. But we can make them available to others simply through repeating them, only by a routine device of language such as has been discussed above. One part of our education is to learn to behave, on receiving such utterances, without adornment, from others, as if we ourselves had had certain experiences; though a later part, doubtless, is to learn to do this with circumspection.

That such utterances may be put to this use obliges us to distinguish two senses of words like " statement " or " description " : first, as referring to a combination of words correlated in the characteristic way with a range of objective situations, and second, as referring to a certain kind of symbol-using activity, wherein by a routine of language we make these combinations available to others in a manner recognized by a given social group. But a third sense must be distinguished, for there is a grammatical form characteristic of this linguistic routine as of others, and, as also in other cases, the grammatical form (indicative verbs and the rest) may occur in utterances serving purposes other than its characteristic purpose. Such an utterance is often called a *statement* merely for grammatical reasons; and so three senses of that word must be distinguished, as indicating a correlation to objects (given the language-habits of a particular group), a use or function of language, and a grammatical form respectively. In the sentence " his statement consisted of three statements, and the last statement was meaningless ", the word occurs first in the second, then (if we ignore what follows) in the first, then in the third sense.

Some of the factors that encourage the utterance of word combinations in statement form have not yet been mentioned. Once the form has been explicitly recognized, we may utter (in particular, write) such combinations for purposes of a literary kind : our purpose is to make something of a certain sort, a verbal complex that, according to the language-habits of a certain group, correlates with a certain arrangement of objects. This is the activity which produces schoolboys' descriptive compositions. Finally, it is likely that philosophers will produce combinations chiefly of this kind, when their purpose is to make something which shall be a specimen of using language — not, be it noted, a specimen of statement, but of using language in any form. Why this should be so is easy to see. The philosopher tries to invent an example of a symbol-complex, when he has no straightforward use for one, but only a use which is indirect and sophisticated — that it should be a philosopher's specimen. He has no intention to promise, or command, or move his reader's feelings ; his eye glances round his room, falls on this or that object, and he says " the table is brown ", or " here is a penny ", or " today is Tuesday and tomorrow is Wednesday ". What else is to be expected of him ? His position, in respect of the utterance he takes as a specimen, is not unlike that of a man who talks without a purpose in talking, or who seeks about for a topic of conversation, regardless of what it may be. It is not to be wondered at that he should bring out the same kind of utterance.

Thus philosophers tend to choose, as their specimens,

utterances of a distinctive kind. Two factors have apparently combined, however, to encourage them in the belief that this distinctive kind of utterance was typical of all utterance. First, sentences with simply the grammatical form of a statement constitute a large variety of utterances where the purpose of making available to others a combination of words correlated with objects in the known manner (that is, the purpose of stating or describing) — is either subordinated to other purposes, or not present at all. Thus the varieties of the use of language are concealed by the diffusion of the indicative mood. Second, genuine statement-utterances play a relatively large part in the lives of philosophers, as of scholars and men of learning generally, and other kinds of utterance a relatively minor part; so that in supposing statement to be typical of utterance, they give a less distorted picture of their own lives than of those of men in general. But that this supposition distorts the facts is undeniable, for to accept it is to think that the peculiar, the distinguishing characteristic of the utterances that philosophers take as specimens, is actually what they have in common with all other forms of utterance. If we accept this view we invert the truth; we assume that what makes one kind of utterance different from other kinds is what makes all the kinds similar.

It is very largely the conviction that statement is the typical activity of utterance which has confused discussions of the problem of meaning. One might argue that it is permissible to study the meaning of an utterance, either in the sense of the correlation between the word-complex comprising it and the objective conditions, or in the sense of its purpose for a given speaker; and that philosophers were entitled to confine their attention to what might be called the question of objective meaning, if they chose. So they would be entitled; but many of those anxious to claim the privilege of choosing this question have really turned to another. Falsely supposing that the basic element in all utterance was statement, they have turned to the question how utterances could have meaning in the sense of being intelligent; and have answered by showing that that basic element was present in a special way: the utterance was correlated with objective conditions by the medium of special mental entities.   But that an activity of uttering is intelligent can be known only if its purpose is known.   If the purpose of uttering were not always to state, this account of how uttering can be intelligent simply could not be true.   Since it is not always to state, it is not true.

CHAPTER IX

AMBIGUITY IN LANGUAGE

THIS chapter examines in greater detail the correlation between utterances and what were called, above, their "objective" conditions. It does so, first, with respect to the objective conditions of particular descriptive words. By the conditions stimulating utterances is now meant, therefore, the objects to which in ordinary speech these utterances are said to refer. The connexion between verbal responses and this restricted range of stimulating conditions shows, more clearly than ever, the close analogy between verbal response, and response of other kinds; in that everything within a range of stimulating conditions will produce, more or less, the same response.

This range of stimulating conditions is comprised of particular conditions that are like each other; but it is important to notice that this likeness is not simple but complex. Of four objects A, B, C, and D, which all evoke the same verbal response, say X, A may have properties p, q, r; B, q, r, s; C, p, s; D, r, s, t. Moreover, these properties may be present in varying degrees; the use of the verbal expression is determined by an unconscious, inconstant reference to and selection from them. Sometimes one analogy is of decisive importance, sometimes another. Finally, the set of influential properties is not closed but open. It will always be possible for further experience so to intertwine some further property, say v, with those already operative, that at length its presence will be of importance in determining whether the verbal response will be made.

137

Nor does this flexibility result only in expansion. The set of operative properties may be diminished if one of its members should cease in practice to be associated with the others. If, for example, the speaker ceases to find objects in which the property q occurs with all or any of p, r, s, and t, his responsiveness to q in this respect will lapse. The ultimate effect of the changes might be to associate the given response with p, r, s, t, v. The meanings we give our words tend to change before we reach the stage of formulating definitions. In respect of the expression " school uniform ", for instance, the property of being prescribed in a school prospectus becomes relevant after a time, and that of resembling the uniform of one's own school ceases progressively to be so. We are not concerned, yet, with how these tendencies are formulated into criteria of usage; only with how they operate even when unformulated.

It is in this way that the use of most words for objects, qualities, or relations is uncertain and unsettled; and their meanings consequently vague. They are employed within a certain range of differing though similar experiences; the similarity may be of more than one kind, and similarity in any one respect is seldom decisive. Moreover, a new type of similarity, either absent hitherto, or merely unnoticed, may at any time become influential, or the influence of another sort of similarity partially or wholly disappear. These uncertainties result from the variety and the continuity of our experience. It is comparatively rare for us to have experiences either identical with, or wholly different from, a given experience or type of experience. Given any one, we soon encounter others which are modifications of it; and given any two, encounter others which are somehow intermediate. In certain cases, admittedly, this occurs only at the recondite level of investigation of the scientist; and when this is so, the boundaries of word-usage appear to be sharp. This applies to some words

for prime movers, like " electricity "; those for some
chemical elements and compounds like " oxygen " or
" water "; and those for the contents of the various
senses, like " sights ", " sounds ", " smells ", and so on
(though between smell and taste the distinction is perhaps
less clear). But even in these cases it is possible at least
to imagine experiences where we should hesitate to say
that a word was apt, or which of two words was apter ;
and often enough, systematic investigation can actually
discover anomalies of the sort to make us hesitate. Clear
boundaries to usage are contingent, and usually not
permanent.

This vagueness and fluidity in the use of language is
to be expected from the nature of response in general ; it
accords with the general character of experience. But
perhaps also it is greater than ever, because children learn
language largely through imitating the conversation of
adults, and not merely in simplified, specially provided
lessons. Thus, all the time, children learn from those
whose experience is far wider than their own, who are
conscious of both similarities and differences of which
children are unaware, and whose linguistic skill is relatively
elaborate. The specializations of a long tradition of litera-
ture, poetry, and metaphor are brought to bear on the
child's simple and highly repetitive experience. He is so
influenced by his intercourse with others that he habitually
performs what are in fact daring linguistic experiments,
before he is much acquainted with a gradual and systematic
extension of usage. He learns, for example, to speak of a
bed for a cat, or for flowers, of the birds going to bed,
perhaps of the bed of the sea, before he even sees more
than two or three objects that are beds in the plain sense.
Similarly, he learns to use many generic words before he
has learnt all or indeed many of the specific words whose
meanings they comprehend.

Another perhaps even more important result of how we

learn is that, at every stage of development, verbal resources tend to be richer and more varied than practical purposes require. We learn a wide variety of verbal expressions which we acquire habits of uttering in response to more or less similar experiences. Each of these expressions is acquired more or less independently. On being shown even so simple an object as a chair, we may say " this is a chair ", or " this is an article of furniture ", or " this is made of wood ", or " this is comprised of legs, a seat, and a back ", or " this is meant to be sat on ", or " this is what my brother sits on at breakfast time ", or " this is hard, brown, and angular ". Each is equally apt ; each expression is acquired as a response to the sort of situation which consists of seeing a chair ; and the list is neither exhaustive nor, probably, capable of exhaustion. Nor, one should notice, is it built up from synonyms, like, for example, the list " this is a sailor . . . a mariner . . . a seafarer . . . a jack-tar ", etc. ; it consists of independent words, expressions, turns of phrase and constructions, each with uses of its own, but each associated with the other, because all are equally appropriate for describing a single experience.

There is no necessary connexion between this feature of our language and that other feature of insistent and general vagueness discussed above. It is relatively easy to construct a language in which either occurred without the other. If, for example, we made a select list of words, taking only one from chosen pages of a *Duden* illustrative dictionary, and using it only by reference to the illustrations, we should probably be able to construct a language with vague meanings (because the boundaries of usage were uncertain and flexible), but without overlapping of meanings. Conversely, if we constructed a perfectly exact vocabulary for describing some suitable activity such as cards or chess, and then invented further expressions to be identical in use with each of the original set or with combinations of them, we should have a language without vagueness, but in which meanings would overlap. In this language, it would be proper to respond to a given situation in any or all of several different ways; but it would differ from our own language, in that the alternatives would be exact equivalents.

If the language of everyday speech conformed to either of these models, we should, however, be at a disadvantage. In the first case, it would not be rich enough for practical requirements; it would be useless, were it to consist only of one word for some aspect of circuses, one for some aspect of music, one for some aspect of carpentry, and so on. In the second, language would be unstable. Anomalous cases, which we did not know how to describe in the precise vocabulary, would constantly occur; and there would be a steady pressure either to invent new, vague expressions, or to blur the existing sharp outlines. That language manifests both these features, however, each to a very considerable degree, has an important consequence.

It was noticed earlier that an expression was normally used not in a sharp and precise manner, but over an unsettled range of situations which resembled each other in one or more of an unsettled number of respects. The first step in crystallizing the usage is by no means to give an authoritative definition of the term; but only to adumbrate its scope, by producing verbal descriptions of the relevant similarities, one after another. Thus in the case of the four objects, A, B, C, and D, discussed above, we should begin to explain or describe how we used " X " if we said that X's had, or tended to have, the property p, or that they tended to have the property q, and so on. None of these observations would exhaustively describe the usage of " X ", nor would there be any limit to their number, or neatly closed set. But they would constitute *criteria*, of an impromptu and inconclusive sort, for the given expression. New relevant criteria might always arise as a result of experience; and conversely, criteria might simply become irrelevant. Furthermore, each criterion could be more or less adequately satisfied, and there would be no rigid boundary between the instances which passed and those which failed. But at all events, we should have equipped ourselves, in formulating a criterion of use, with an explicit and more or less helpful guide.

Some examples will show how criteria of usage might be formulated one after another. Suppose that the application of the word " ripe " to fruit is considered. In the first place, there is a tendency to call red fruit ripe, and fruit which is not red, unripe. When this tendency is verbalized, we have a preliminary criterion; some ripe fruit, however, does not turn red, but resembles red ripe fruit by being sweet. Being sweet constitutes a second and largely independent criterion. Other fruits never become either sweet or red, but resemble the first, because they have reached their maximum size, or are ready to germinate. Others, like medlars, are eaten when they are past this stage; and this introduces yet further criteria when the various tendencies of usage are put into words. There is no fixed specification, or even fixed set of alternative specifications, to which a fruit must conform if it is to be called ripe; and the possible combinations vary not only in respect of the criteria, but of the varying degrees to which they are satisfied. A fruit, for example, which was outstandingly sweet, might be called ripe even if it satisfied none of the other criteria; but one which was only fairly sweet might need to have its claim reinforced in other ways.

Similarly one could construct a set of criteria for using the word " chair ". These would perhaps refer to the constituent parts of the object (such as legs, a seat, and a back), the substances from which it was made, its general shape and structure, its size, its normal use, and the use to which its maker intended it to be put; and further criteria might always be deliberately introduced, or one might notice that unconsciously they were being followed. Two others which are often important in determining whether or not an object is properly described by a certain word are, first, those other words which are used to describe it, and second, its habits, behaviour, and causal properties — what Locke would have called its " powers ".

These criteria will be produced one after another and be used as guides ; but they are generally inconclusive both positively and negatively. That is to say, although a given object satisfies a certain criterion, the question might always still be raised, whether on other grounds it was not disqualified from being described by the word in question ; and conversely, though it fails to satisfy the criterion, one might argue that even so one could describe it properly by the word. Theoretically, indeed, either of these arguments would be possible, at least for certain classes of word, however many of the criteria produced had been satisfied, or not satisfied.

A significant fact now emerges. These criteria employ some or all of the other descriptions normally applicable when the description in question is applicable ; consequently we were concerned with them, earlier in this chapter, in a different form. Because experience has a certain degree of regularity, it is usually true that if a given expression applies to a situation, others of a known open set will apply also. When, therefore, some uncertainty arises about the first expression, the others that are normally applicable will be tried in an *ad hoc* succession. These other expressions now function as criteria of the aptness of the first ; and if there is less uncertainty about them than about it, they may indicate whether or not it should be used. If a language were so thin in texture that no expressions had overlapping applications, then to formulate our habits of usage as verbal criteria would be impossible.

The use not only of nouns and adjectives, but also of verbs and prepositions exhibits these features. When a court of law is, perhaps, required to decide whether a hotel-manager *neglected* his fire-appliances, or whether a certain person contracted or merely undertook to act in a certain way, it is likely to refer to certain sharp definitions or quasi-definitions (such as the judges' summings-up in precedent cases) which will be discussed later. But if these questions are considered in everyday conversation, the same multiplicity of alternative and inconclusive criteria is discovered, and the same relative uncertainty often ensues. It is less frequently so with prepositions, because their usage is prescribed by a lavish supply of fixed idioms, and so the difficulties of the problem are transferred to the accompanying noun or other word. But the problems do arise if a new expression is to be coined, and with certain at times nearly equivalent prepositions like " by " and " through ".

The effect of this discussion is to show how the *terms* employed in ordinary speech, and therefore the statements which are built up round them, function differently from those employed and constructed in an exact logical calculus. A precise use of words, and in consequence a precise significance for sentences, may be the final state of a systematized language, but is certainly not its initial state in ordinary speech. The next step is to examine such words as " but ", " and ", " if ", " or ", " all ", " some ", and " not "; for these correspond to the logical constants of a calculus, and it is important to know whether they are used just as constants are used.

Clearly they are not. The disparity between these words and the constants in a calculus is as great as that between ordinary empirical-concept words and the terms of a calculus. Words like " but ", " although ", and " yet ", for example, cannot be analysed in terms only of the Russellian constants; it would be necessary to introduce a new concept of "apparent implication". "Although he was ill, he came" differs from "he was ill, and he came", because it suggests that his being ill might be expected to have prevented his coming. This "apparent implication" cannot always be interpreted as a statement about probabilities, because it can be employed to suggest that a connexion, though not realized in fact, is nevertheless *proper*; as, for example, "although you pray for the good of others, you do them only harm". If "apparent implication" were symbolized by [⊃], then "he came, but he was ill" would correspond to "$p . q [⊃] \sim p . q$".

"And", as in fact used, differs in several ways from the " . " of Russellian logic. Sometimes it implies more than conjunction, and is a mild or tentative form of "and therefore" or of "and then" (for example, "and he went out, and wept bitterly", which illustrates both these meanings in succession). In other cases it conjoins in a variety of ways. Consider the sentences:

(i) "That is a flock of rooks and jackdaws."
(ii) "They are twelve good men and true."
(iii) "The characters of this book are sons and lovers."

All these are about all the members of a certain class; but the first asserts that the members have either of two qualities (but not both), the second that they all have both of two qualities, and the third that they have either or both of two qualities. The differences could be illustrated in Russellian symbols:

(i) $(x): x \epsilon A . ⊃ . \sim [\phi x . \psi x] . \sim [\sim \phi x . \sim \psi x]$
(ii) $(x): x \epsilon B . ⊃ . \phi x . \psi x$
(iii) $(x): x \epsilon C . ⊃ . \phi x \lor \psi x$

There are similar disparities between the use of the implication sign in logic and the word "if" in ordinary speech. To some extent the ambiguities in this word are resolved by tense-devices. For example, "if he had come,

L

I should have told him " implies that the protasis is unfulfilled and that the apodosis is therefore unlikely to be fulfilled either; " if that is the case, I shall tell him " implies the contrary, and " if he comes, I shall go " has neither implication. " If he were to . . . " implies that the protasis is not expected to be fulfilled. The three first could be symbolized respectively, " $\sim p . \sim q . p \supset q$ "; " $p . q . p \supset q$ "; " $p \supset q$ ". More important, perhaps, than these differences is the fact that in ordinary language " if " is used indifferently to indicate a logical connexion, and an empirical and contingent association; as in " if an object is a quadrilateral it has four sides ", and " if an object is a church, it has a nave ".

The words " all " and " some " raise similar problems. It is futile for logicians to dispute whether " all " implies the existence of instances of the sort referred to; for in ordinary language the question has not been raised or considered, and therefore no answer has been given, though either may henceforth be adopted. Like " if ", " all " is used for logical and for empirical connexions, which is the same as to say, in deductive and in inductive arguments; and by extension perhaps from this use, it is sometimes legitimate to use " all " even when there are exceptions to the generalization, and " most " would in one sense be apter.

" Some " in ordinary speech cannot be identified either with the " some " of Aristotelian logic, or the $(\exists x)$ sign of Russell. In the first place, conversion is disallowed in certain cases, " some sufferers from foot-and-mouth disease are cattle " having false implications in plain language, for example. In the second, " some " frequently, though not always, suggests not " at least one ", but an appreciable proportion of the whole. Moreover, the magnitude of this proportion may be suggested by the speaker's tone or the verbal context; in certain cases the use of " some " implicitly adds " but not many ", in other

cases it adds " and fairly many ". In addition, " some "
may have connotations of approval or disapproval, and
suggest that the instances of which it is used ought alone
to be regarded, or ought to be ignored. In a language
which was the exact verbal counterpart of a precise calculus (if that were possible) these additional elements would
be expressible only in additional statements ; and this is
true also of that use of " some " where it is like " certain ",
and implies " instances known to you and me, and significant in some way, but about which it is unnecessary or
undesirable to say more ". In ordinary speech the quasi-
logical words lack the diaphanous quality of the logical
particles in a calculus ; they help to carry the sense itself.

The ambiguities connected with " or " are less complex,
but interesting because this word contrasts sharply in
several ways with its formal counterpart in Russell's
terminology. The only possibility excluded by the dis-
junction " $a \lor b$ " is " not-a and not-b ". The use of " or "
is more complex. Suppose, for example, that one of the
conditions in an examination is " candidates may submit
translations from Latin or from Greek ". This statement
may be given any one of four different interpretations :
that they must submit translations from one language and
one only (excluded possibilities, *both*, and *neither*) ; that
they must not submit translations from both languages,
but may submit none at all (excluded possibility, *both*) ;
that they must submit translations from one or other
language, or both (excluded possibility, *neither*) ; and last,
that they are free to submit translations from either
language, or both, or neither, as they prefer. Thus the
ambiguity is complete. We may use " or ", in ordinary
language, either to make any restriction we care to choose,
or to indicate that there are no restrictions whatsoever.

The most varied and complex ambiguities, however,
are exhibited by the word " not " and the other negative
forms such as " un- ". First, these are not always used

like Russell's " $\sim$ ", because they do not always conform to the rule that a double negation returns to the meaning of the original expression ($\sim\sim p \equiv p$); "not unequal to the task" is not equivalent to "equal to the task". Again, a sentence, such as "this is not blue" is entailed by either "this is red and blue" or "this is red and green". In the first case the deduction is based on a principle which, when symbolized, reads "$p . q . \supset . \sim p$" which is incompatible with Russell's logic. Here in fact a distinction is made between "not blue at all" and "not wholly blue". Further distinctions can be traced: for example, a hat which was blue except for a thin red band would be called blue; but if rather more of the hat were coloured otherwise than blue, it might be called "hardly blue", and if none of it were blue, then "not blue at all". In French, alternative forms (*ne . . . guère, ne . . . pas, ne . . . point*) make it possible to introduce these distinctions by the negative itself. But there are other expressions such as "not nearly" in English, which have an intermediate usage.

Thus "not" is far from functioning in ordinary language like the negation-signs of Aristotle's or Russell's logic. It seems truest, indeed, to say that it does duty sometimes for one, sometimes for another, of at least four negative formulae of increasing force: "not quite", "not by any means", "not nearly", and "not at all". To give the closest possible formal analogue to this usage a logic with four negation-signs would be required, and it might be possible to find traces in ordinary language which would indicate what rules would be adopted in interrelating them. On the whole it seems as if a "Law of Excluded Sixth" would represent actual usage more closely than a system in which the stronger forms cumulatively implied the weaker; and the fact that it would on occasion be proper to contradict "that's not quite blue", by "it's not *nearly* not quite blue, it's not blue at all", gives a clue to the appropriate rules for double negation in all its various forms.

Negation in ordinary language can be connected with movement along a scale in another way. Instead of thinking of the negation itself as susceptible of varying degrees, it is sometimes more natural to think of a group of predicates as themselves arranged in a scale. Then, depending upon tone of voice, or verbal context, a negation implies some positive sentence which uses a predicate somewhat further along that scale, or a limited distance less far. The negative works by selection rather than limitation. Thus in certain cases " he is not *old* " would imply that he was middle-aged or at least nearly so, and would be barely compatible with " he is young ". Alternatively " he is not lazy " might imply that he was more than lazy, and actually vicious. These uses can be made explicit by such expressions as " I wouldn't go so far as to say that . . .", or " not really " ; and by " not simply ". To symbolize them we should have to adopt the notion of a progressive set of predicates, $\phi_1, \phi_2, \phi_3 \ldots \phi_n \ldots$; then for the first form of negation $\sim \phi_n a \supset \phi_{n-\delta} a$, where δ is fairly small, and for the second $\sim \phi_n a \supset \phi_{n+\delta} a$. Colour-propositions exhibit both this use of " not ", and that discussed in the last paragraph : " it's not *red* " may mean equally " it is nearly red " or " it is brilliant scarlet ". Sometimes a set of alternative predicates is available, sometimes only several degrees of negation ; often we use a mixture of both.

" Not " can also be used loosely in a manner which is the counterpart of the loose meaning of " all ". " I don't smoke " may simply mean " I don't often smoke ". Negating a sentence which has a dispositional predicate sometimes means that the object never behaves in the manner in question, and is sometimes only preparatory to giving a condition in which the disposition will after all be manifested. If the condition given is one of what might be termed " maximum frequency ", then the negation is rendered absurd; as in " I don't smoke except when I want to " or " this plant does not flower except in the spring and summer ". But when the condition is seldom satisfied, as in " this plant does not flower except in very wet summers ", then the negation is intelligible and legitimate. By this means we have a distinction between " not ever " and " not often ".

It is interesting to notice that these two alternative meanings may be expressed explicitly, either by adopting one or the other forms of negation, or by modifying the dispositional predicate itself. Thus " he is fairly conventional " and " he is not often unconventional ", " this plant occasionally flowers " and " this plant does not often flower ", are equivalent in meaning. Sometimes, as with " stable " and " inert " in chemistry, even adverbs are superfluous, for there is more than one dispositional predicate, indicating the varying frequency with which the disposition is suspended or implying that it is without exception. Sometimes the particular way in which the disposition is limited can also be given, as in " the swallow is a summer migrant "; for this is equivalent to " the swallow comes to this country only in summer ", and therefore to " the swallow does not come to this country except in summer ". That this partial or conditional negation can be concealed in a sentence which is apparently only positive in form emphasizes that the " not . . . except . . ." or " not . . . unless . . ." expression must be interpreted as a single whole; and this in turn shows how the negation is quite different in meaning from that of the logical constant sometimes equated with it.

These features of the use of " not ", " if ", and the rest would still be of some importance, were they overt and explicit alternative meanings; but in common speech they are not. An ordinary speaker has never considered how he uses these words on different occasions; though if challenged he would find himself driven sometimes to

elucidate his utterances in one way, sometimes in another.
His expressions are not ambiguous because they are
equivocal, but because they are simply indeterminate.
Consequently others will simply not know how to interpret
them beyond a certain level of precision ; and if the speaker
attempts to discover himself, he ceases to use his language
uncritically and has begun to philosophize over it.

There is a second disadvantage to the indeterminate
character of common language.   It was seen that the
criteria of whether a given description was appropriate to
a given case were some of the other descriptions normally
applicable when the first is applicable.   This joint appropriateness induces a tendency to assert either, if the other
has already been accepted ;   and at a level of greater
systematization, to infer either from the other, depending
upon which, in the given case, is accepted first.   But such
inference is invalidated by vagueness and flexibility in
the meanings of the empirical-concept words, and also by
indeterminacy in the uses of the logical words.   Deduction
in the language of everyday speech is like manipulating a
logical calculus in which there are no constant rules of
inference, and the Law of Identity is invalid.   This is not
merely a disadvantage because deductive methods, where
they are possible, are useful ;   it is doubly dangerous because
using language naturally sets up (by the Law of Success)
habits of making verbal transitions which follow deductive
patterns, even if these are not based on the recognition of
logical connexions.

A third disadvantage is that even when the inferred
propositions prove to be not false, they are likely to be
true only in some new sense.   For example, in the normal
domestic routine the word " bed " has a certain fairly
well-defined usage, and so have such associated expressions
as " in bed ", " under the bed ", " to make a bed ", and
so on.   But if the word " bed " is extended in use until it
can be applied to a patch of ground where a soldier throws

himself down to sleep with his coat over him and his pack for a pillow, then the meanings of these other expressions will change or even disappear. Since their significance depends in turn on those other expressions which can be employed if they can be employed, and therefore inferred from them, this is really another way of saying that even if we avoid false inferences at the first remove, we encounter them at the second.

These disadvantages all point in the direction of obtaining a more precise language by introducing a greater degree of systematization. The next chapter will examine the attempt to do so and how it fares.

CHAPTER X

LANGUAGE AS A SYSTEM

THE last chapter argued that a verbal response may be stimulated by any situation within a fairly wide range; and that the limits of this range are unsettled and variable. But a response, verbal or otherwise, may be inhibited as well as stimulated. The criteria of inappropriateness are often as influential as those of appropriateness, sometimes more so. This is clearly true of negative adjectives like those beginning with " un- " or " in- "; but it is equally true of many words where this element is entirely implicit, like " neat " (of spirits), " scalene ", or " original ". These negative or inhibiting conditions, however, are no less complex, unco-ordinated, and *ad hoc* in their application than the positive; and situations can arise in which an indefinite number of indecisive partial stimuli tend to produce a certain response, and another indefinite number of indecisive partial stimuli tend to inhibit it.

Situations of this sort relating to non-verbal behaviour have often been investigated under laboratory conditions. In animals they produce weak or hesitant responses; or, if they occur too frequently, unresponsiveness and hysteria. In speech, a weak response means a whisper; but whispering, though it could be the means of indicating that the situation was anomalous, has obvious disadvantages. A special device is needed which shows that we are concerned with a border-line case, but leaves us free to respond clearly and distinctly. The simplest critical development of language, in contrast to the spontaneous extension of usage, seems to be introducing phrases to show that we find our utterances only just appropriate to the facts. We have a variety of such expressions : " a sort of . . ." ; " more or less . . ." ; " a special . . ." ; " a modified . . ." ; " not a real . . ." ; " a seeming . . ." ; " really more than just a . . ." ; " an occasional . . ." ; " in part . . ." ; " from one point of view . . ." ; " to some extent . . ." ; " not entirely un- . . ." ; ". . . -ish ", and many others. In contrast to these, expressions like " true . . ." ; " a perfect . . ." ; " genuine . . ." ; or " a typical . . ." display particular confidence that our expression is apt.

Alternatively, one may transgress the Law of Contradiction and say " it is and it isn't ". A visitor to a certain house might describe his reception as both cordial and not cordial ; or a man might say that he wanted something but that " then again " he did not. Such remarks often precede a redescription employing a fuller vocabulary ; but this is not essential for them to be intelligible. It means something to be told that an action was and was not polite, though it may be a second best ; and to be told that a medicine bottle contains a special sedative, or a sort of poison, is more useful than to be told nothing, and far more useful than to be told that it is the one, or is the other, without qualification. These expressions, that seem as if they only blur our language, really make it in one sense more precise ; for they increase the proportion of occasions in which we can describe our experiences without distortion. They make language more subtle and its potentialities more varied. Verbal counters are in any case related flexibly and variably ; but if ever that should be insufficient, these supplementary expressions provide means of speaking more flexibly still.

These devices partly remove the first disadvantage inherent in ordinary language. They make the looseness of its usage explicit ; and so they warn the hearer that the

speaker may be employing a word as he would not himself
have expected. But they do nothing to validate inference.
This requires that the language of speech should conform
to the pattern of a calculus ; there must be precise definitions of both its logical words and its empirical concepts.
The systematization of language involves, above all, processes of definition.

The word " definition " will be employed to refer to
any process making more precise the limits within which
a word may be used. This may be effected in various
ways. First, one may give verbal equivalents, either
directly of the word itself, or indirectly of a sentence or of
sentences in which it occurs. But it is likely that no single
phrase, and in particular no single genus-species phrase,
will be sufficient ; and ultimately this method is dependent
on other methods. One of these is to describe, in words
or pictures, a situation to which the original word is applicable ; but in principle this description could always be
replaced by an instance, or more properly a complex set
of instances, illustrating the whole range of meaning.

Thus of these three methods the second is reducible
to the third (and perhaps to the first also) ; and the first
and third are of chief importance. The third method is
that commonly referred to as " ostensive definition ". It
was originally introduced to define only a small and special
class of words ; for philosophers believed that the definition
of the word epitomized the essence of that universal or
concept for which the word stood, but saw no way of
epitomizing or redescribing an essence which was perfectly
simple. Such a concept could be referred to only by its
own name, and in any instance of it there was nothing
but the universal made particular. In a patch of magenta,
for example, there were no inessential qualities for a verbal
definition to exclude, and the essential quality could either
be referred to by the word " magenta " itself, or by exact
synonyms, or not at all. But the meaning of " magenta "

still required to be given, since no one could persuade himself that it was self-evident; and therefore it was allowed that this be done by producing an instance. Words which referred to simple and unanalysable qualities could therefore be defined ostensively, and others with more complex meanings by a process of analysing the meanings into their simple constituents.

This method seemed the more plausible, because it was supposed that although the meaning of a generic word might consist of a set of alternative possibilities ("coloured" for example, meaning "either red or blue or green . . ."), words for simple qualities like single shades of colour were quite unequivocal. A word like "magenta" had a perfectly specific meaning; all magenta patches were absolutely identical; therefore, producing any one of them told the whole story about magenta. But realizing that three shades could be found, such that although the first and second and the second and third were indistinguishable, yet the first and third could be distinguished, threw doubt on these beliefs, and set the process of ostensive definition in a new light. For it suggested that even specific colour-words had a "fringe" of uncertainty, although their range of meaning might be narrow. Nor can this difficulty be avoided by saying that a specific colour-word means "that which is common to all patches indistinguishable from each other and from this given patch", and presenting a particular colour-patch, since it is sometimes impossible to decide whether two patches are indistinguishable in colour or not; and as a corollary, sometimes impossible to decide whether the colour of a given patch really seems homogeneous — in other words, to say what is and what is not a patch of colour.

Thus even in the case of a word so restricted in meaning as a specific colour-word, ostensive definition does not present an essence, but illustrates a range of usage, and a range, moreover, with uncertain boundaries. A more subtle study of colours indicates that this range extends in directions quite ignored by the original simple analysis. Colours which are identical in shade may differ in quality; slightly, but in several ways. The empty blue of the sky, the almost palpably spongy yellow of a distant haze seen from mountains, the crimson depths of a glass of wine, the ubiquitous but elusive green of water seen from beneath its surface, the colours of jewels or of glowing metal or a brilliant light, differ not only in shade but also in other less conspicuous qualities.[1] The shades could be identical and these other differences remain. Although they are not prominent, and they chiefly interest artists, writers, and psychologists, there are certain fairly crude methods for distinguishing them verbally. A particular shade of colour may have a *lustre* or a *sheen*; it may be a *gloss* or a *bloom*; it may *glow*, or *glare*, or *dazzle*, or sometimes even *dance*; we may speak of crimson *depths*, or the *empty* blue of the sky.

Clearly, therefore, even the simplest ostensive definitions map a range of uses, and even for the simplest and most specific words, two conclusions are certain. The first is that the ideal ostensive definition requires more than one sample (though perhaps only a small set); the second is that no such definition can be entirely final and exhaustive, for some new distinction or new variety might always be discovered later.

But if complexity and persistent vagueness are both provided for in an ostensive definition, then other more complex types of words can be ostensively defined. To achieve this it will be necessary only to increase the number and variety of the illustrative examples, and in so doing to leave a greater field for extending the use of the word in a greater number of directions, or a more extensive borderland of uncertainty and freedom.

The scope of ostensive definition is thus wider than

[1] I am indebted for the gist of this remark to Dr. F. Waismann.

has been supposed. It is not restricted to simple and immediately sensible quality-words ; it is equally applicable to generic words like " coloured " or even " sensible ". That the range of use is wider and the definition not exhaustive in more numerous ways does not affect the principle. More important, perhaps, material-object words can be ostensively defined. In order to define a word like " tree " ostensively, for a person who understands what any ostensive definition is, it is necessary only to produce a series of examples — a series of situations in which it is appropriate to use the word " tree ".

In the course of such a process, one difficulty might arise. One of the examples might prove to be not a real tree, but an illusion or a piece of camouflage ; and this would make it seem as if sentences expressing definitions could be false. But this paradox is easily avoided. First, it is not the case that definitions cannot be false because they must be true ; they cannot be false because when a verbal activity is classified as *defining*, it is classified as something to which neither " true " nor " false " is applicable. Consequently to apply either of these terms signifies that the activity is no longer being interpreted as a definition, but as an assertion ; and if this is done, nothing is easier than that, on other definitions, it should prove to be false. Second, a specimen which misleads in this way will satisfy some of the relevant criteria, but proves subsequently not to satisfy others : it constitutes, perhaps, an experience which has a tree-like appearance, but not a tree-like permanence. But that this subsequent surprise can occur is another proof that all the criteria of usage are not formulated at once ; and this in turn shows once more that they are several, and that fresh criteria may always be added.

Words which cannot be ostensively defined singly and directly can be defined indirectly, if sentences are constructed which include them, and then we are progressively shown the sorts of situation in which it is appropriate to use these sentences for one determined purpose or another. In this way it is possible to illustrate the meanings not only of many abstract nouns, but also of the logical words. This would often involve the exhibition of changing processes, but so after all would ostensively defining " explosion " or " blush ". The meanings of " not " or " all " could indirectly be given by presenting situations of which sentences like " all the birds have flown away " or " there is no cheese on the table " were appropriate descriptions. Even words like " here " and " this " can be given indirect ostensive definitions of a kind; though the set of illustrative examples must show the significant part played by the speaker's body, and the insignificance of surrounding objects; and, as indeed with all words defined by constructing and applying sentences, we present not something to which the word refers, but instances of its proper use.

" Defining " in this sense is closely linked with the normal method of learning and teaching a vocabulary; and it would be strange if such ostensive definitions were impossible, for they are simply emphatic and ritualized analogues of ordinary usage. If an adult tries to define, say, " drawing ", or " house " ostensively, for a child, he uses the word intensively for a limited period, in as varied and comprehensive a manner as he can. For the child, three months' experience of hearing the word in casual conversation may be compressed into as many minutes. Our language-habits are normally conditioned and our vocabulary extended through imitation, because others constantly though unconsciously provide exemplars; ostensive definition merely concentrates this process. That is why it parallels ordinary usage in its incompleteness. A new range of samples, or an intermediate sample, may always be added, or the samples regrouped, just as in ordinary speech the use of words way be extended, either by introducing fresh criteria (or their application to a new case), or by spontaneously extending a response.

This association between ostensively defining and ordinarily using a word, however, means that the ostensive form of definition will not suffice to eradicate the difficulties about deduction. Ostensive definition is a deliberate and comprehensive attempt to produce the whole range of usage, and will therefore illustrate a whole set of criteria which are partial alternatives and not complementaries. Even if a restriction is introduced, and an attempt made both to make the range homogeneous and to delimit it exactly, the risk of uncertainty in usage remains. Some quite novel experience is always likely to occur, and be such that it is distinctively different from those which already illustrate the meaning, but yet at the same time is not to be excluded from the class. Conversely, a more subtle approach may always discover an ambiguity already present in the defining set : some difference among the accepted group of samples, significant enough to deserve recognition, but obscured and glossed over by the existing definition. While the meaning of a word is fixed by relating it to facts, the risk of ambiguity, both at the periphery of existing use and within it, can be reduced but never removed.

Ostensive definition, therefore, does not enable us to treat the verbal language as a logical calculus. This requires that the interrelations between the verbal constituents shall be prescribed without remainder ; and ostensive definition will always leave a remainder. Only by defining one word in terms of others can its relation to them, and therefore to those in which they are defined, be made thoroughly determinate. Besides this, the operations and functions of the logical words must also be exactly fixed. But these two demands are not ultimately separable. When the rules of operating " not ", " or ", " all ", and the rest are determined for all expressions, the interrelations of the terms with which they are used will be completely defined.

For example, such a principle as " no part of a coloured expanse can at a given instant be both red and blue " is significant in two different ways. On the one hand it is (from the premiss " red is not blue ") an application of the Law of Contradiction; and as such it insists that " and " and " not " shall be used in a certain way. But it also begins to define " part ", " instant ", " red ", and " blue ", and to do so each in terms of the other (as may be required) by prescribing how sentences containing some of these terms shall entail or exclude sentences containing others. For example, a given shade of mauve might be indistinguishable from shades comprised under both the genus-word " red " and the genus-word " blue ". Then it would appear, *prima facie*, that the shade was both red and blue; but the dictum forbids us to define our terms so that this problem could arise. Alternatively, it opposes using " part " vaguely; it condemns, for example, an expression like " the upper part of the square was red and blue ", and claims that " part " should be defined in terms of colour-homogeneity or *minima visibilia*, and used precisely. Similarly " every coloured expanse is either red or not red " insists on certain usages for (in effect) " all ", " or ", and " not " when used in respect of colour expanses, and thereby insists on a meaning for " red " sufficiently precise to make these logical rules workable.

The " Law of Excluded Middle " has as its most prominent function to prescribe an exact use for " not "; but it is only a special form of a more general principle. This more general principle has a pervasive influence on the vocabulary of language. It is that every classificatory scheme shall be exhaustive. Persons travelling on a ship, for example, are classified as ship's officers, crew, first-class passengers, second-class passengers, steerage passengers, or stowaways. Revenue is from taxation, borrowing,

M

government enterprises . . . or miscellaneous sources.   A
Minister is either the Minister of Labour, or of Education, or . . . a Minister of State.   The expenditure of
a firm is on raw materials, wages, equipment . . . or
sundries.   Anything which cannot be placed under one of
the specific heads does not qualify for the generic title
either, for generic and specific expressions are mutually
defined.   This mutual definition gives precise interrelations
between the terms, and the whole vocabulary can thus be
treated as part of an exact calculus.   In a special case where
none of the particular words are applicable, but there is a
desire to use the general word, some further category will
be invented, using expressions like " quasi- ", " apparent ",
or " alleged ".

But when this occurs, the categorial scheme is only pre-
tending to be precise and exhaustive.   What appears to be
a genuine category is in one case only a vague portmanteau-
term, giving us latitude to include in the genus any and
every particular that we have no reason to include except
a wish to do so.   The miscellaneous books in a library are
those which the librarian wants on his shelves, but cannot
classify properly.   A stowaway is anybody on board a
ship not falling under any of the definable heads.   A
Minister of State is anybody, regardless of his work and
duties, whom the Prime Minister pleases to call a Minister.
The main divisions in a scheme apparently require, if they
themselves are to be exact, a further division, which can
include anything however strange and unexpected, because
unlike them it is left as vague as possible.

Why a vague counterpart to a precise vocabulary is
essential has already been discussed.   The equipment for
description can always be somewhat in advance of experience, because we may always supplement experience by
imagining possible but hitherto unobserved varieties, and
preparing for their advent.   But this extrapolation is
limited in scope.   We may always be surprised by a novelty

outside the existing range of experience, or by a subtlety
within it. By interrelating terms through mutual definition, we may sharpen the outlines of a language, but we
coarsen its texture. The unsystematized usage could fit
snugly to the facts, whatever these proved to be, by virtue
of its viscosity. By crystallizing usage, a finite gap is
created between each expression and its neighbours, and
the possibility arises of an occurrence which defies the
descriptive equipment. An additional category under
which every anomalous case may be set is therefore
required. A parallel might be drawn with the process of
reproducing a picture by drawing a grid over it, and taking
the predominant colour in each square of the grid as its
only colour. By increasing the fineness of the mesh, the
original can be transcribed with less and less distortion;
but a picture might always be discovered of which some
part conformed so little to the contours of the predetermined
grid, that it was better to suspend its use, and copy freehand.

If in systematizing language we do not specially
provide expressions with an elastic and comprehensive use,
the consequences are remarkable. Mutual verbal definitions are constructed by formulating, with alleged complete
adequacy, the criteria for use of a given word; and since
this is so, they provide interlocking criteria both for the
key-word itself, and for those which occur in its definition.
Thus a limited area of our vocabulary is made determinate,
each part of it in terms of the others. But no such area is
entirely self-sufficient. Since the original set of criteria,
now formalized into a definition, was an open set, but the
definition is closed, some of the original tendencies of use
must be passed over; and similarly, the words used to
construct the criteria (though their usage is itself partly
determined by reference to the key-word) were at the less
systematized level also linked to words outside the defined
circle. Thus this defined vocabulary is always under the
influence of other tendencies of usage, linking its elements

to the rest of the language. These tendencies are not accorded recognition, and they could not exhaustively be recognized; but their influence is felt whenever an anomalous case reveals the strain put upon usage by the defining process. When this happens, one of two consequences ensues. If, by virtue of the definitions, a word is denied application although there are strong unrecognized forces making it applicable, then the significance of the denial tends to evanesce. If, conversely, the word is applied in spite of forces strongly against its application, then the application seems to prize the word up and away from a snug conformity to the facts; its use seems artificial; the essential features of the situation seem to have escaped again. In short, when a set of words with precise definitions is applied to a situation which does not humour this exactitude, the definitions are stultified, and there is an elusive change of meaning after all.

These changes do not conform to a regular pattern, for if they were to do so, a routine provision could be made for them. Each case has its own features, and the best method of revealing their character is to give examples. Let us consider first the dictum mentioned above: " no single part of a coloured expanse can be both red and blue ". There is a difficulty about applying this to speckled surfaces when the speckle appears particularly fine; its application depends in the long run on insisting that every *minimum visibile* is treated as a distinct part. But to do so involves using " part " so that we are obliged to speak of spatial parts which cannot be counted and which do not have parts themselves; and none of the normal criteria for " being extended " or " having shape " apply, since the parts are only visible points of light. The only justification for speaking of their extension or shape is that we insist that they (and indeed they alone) are properly describable as parts; and that there is a quite independent formula which associates " part ", " shape ", and " extension ".

Everything except the formula associating " part " and " homogeneously coloured " argues against the claim that each uncountable and unisolatable speckle was a part. We may allow a decisive influence to this formula, and therefore use the word; but the significance of using it fades away, if it is to bring none of its usual implications. A similar result follows from applying the related formula, " everything coloured is extended ", to a coloured point of light (like a small star on a very clear night). Here " extension " becomes vapid; its use is rejected by everything but the formula. The descriptive force of the expression, applied to a point of light, is nil; and the factual element vanishes from our assertion, because the assertion is only a display of loyalty to the rubric.

Again, the use of " know " is sometimes prescribed by saying that " I know p but I may be wrong " is self-contradictory. If this formula is accepted, it becomes true that I cannot know, not merely empirical propositions, but any propositions at all; for I may always make mistakes in deduction, or find self-evident something which is not self-evident, or use the wrong word to describe an immediate experience, because my memory fails. But a denial on these grounds that there is any knowledge empties " knowledge " of significance; for it gives no fresh information about what we called our knowledge and constitutes only a demand that the formula should be accepted as overriding. " Just as you wish ", we feel tempted to reply, " there may be no *knowledge*, if that is what it is to mean. But there are still several sorts of knowledge in all the important respects."

Suppose that, in an attempt to avoid reference to material substance because this expression seems to denote something unobservable and metaphysical, we argue that sentences about material objects really mean sets of sentences about actual or possible experiences. Then if we wish to explain a certain event by drawing attention to the causal influence of an unobserved object, we shall have to explain the existence, and presence, of this unobserved object in terms only of possible experiences. At this point an objection might be raised. " If when you speak of an unobserved object," it might be said, " you speak only of a set of possible experiences, how have you introduced anything upon which an actual event can causally depend? Actual events cannot depend on possible causes."[1] Here the ambiguity is breaking out at more points than one; and it is this which empties the objection of any force. For if it is legitimate to maintain that a material object is a set of possible experiences (which might more cogently be objected to), and therefore by definition a set of possibilities, and therefore only a possible object, nevertheless, " possible " is here used in a new sense. It is used quite differently from " possible " in " he mentioned several possible causes, but none proved to be the cause ". That actual events cannot depend on possible causes, in the original sense of this expression, does not prove that they cannot in the new sense which it has in the expression " possible object " meaning collection of possible experiences. Or one could reply " perhaps the effect cannot *depend* on an unobserved object, if this is a set of possible experiences; but it can do something which is like depending in all important respects ". One may say either that " possible " was being used abnormally, but thereby permitted the use of " depend on " in a normal sense; or that " possible " occurred in a normal sense, and " depend on " abnormally.

Let us take as a third example the assertion " all *a priori* propositions are verbal ". It is sometimes pointed out that as " *a priori* ", " verbal ", and " empirical " are normally inter-defined, this would imply that all *a priori*

[1] Cf. H. H. Price, *Perception* (1932), chap. ix, and W. F. R. Hardie, " The Paradox of Phenomenalism ", *Proceedings of the Aristotelian Society*, 1945–46.

propositions were empirical; for verbal propositions are about the empirical facts of linguistic usage. This is an interesting example, because the loss of significance can be seen at two stages. "All *a priori* propositions are verbal" is itself not an empirical proposition, or intended to be. As far as it is an assertion at all, it must be deduced from definitions of the expressions used; and adherence to this scheme of definitions creates a certain linguistic strain. It may in some sense be true that *a priori* propositions are verbal, but even so they differ in important respects from typically verbal propositions. This, though, is only half the story. To say conversely that *a priori* propositions are *not* verbal, creates a contrary strain. For it too emphasizes certain criteria of usage at the expense of others with a good claim to consideration; and in doing so it refuses to recognize an important though not perhaps easily describable similarity between typically *a priori* and admittedly verbal propositions.

Having recourse to the second formula "all verbal propositions are empirical" accentuates the tendency. For if empirical propositions are to include all *a priori* propositions, then the meaning of "empirical" is surreptitiously extended exactly enough to rob the assertion of any force. But the assertion that no *a priori* propositions are empirical does not constitute a denial of the facts to which the contrary statement drew attention; it merely rejects a certain manner of expressing them. Once again a denial does not deny the substance, but only the phrasing of the argument; the person denying introduces only a *nominal* change, and sooner or later goes on to say the same thing afresh in his own words.

Again, "being significant" or "having meaning" is often defined, as regards empirical statements, in terms of being verifiable; and often it seems straightforwardly true that a sentence which is, if anything, empirical, but not verifiable, is indeed without significance. In other cases, the assertion that a sentence has no meaning because it is unverifiable loses its force; extending the principle to apply it in this instance restricts the significance of " has no meaning " so that although it retains its connexion with unverifiability, it misses the important features of the given sentence.

Hume's argument about induction, and the most frequent refutation of it, follow the same pattern. He argues that an assertion must be proved either by deduction or inductively. But that inductive argument really constitutes proof cannot be proved deductively, as it involves a reference to matters of fact, and cannot be proved inductively, as this would beg the question. Therefore the principle cannot be proved at all; and as rational belief is belief in provable propositions, belief in induction is not rational. This last assertion, however, surreptitiously extends the meaning of " rational "; for Hume here utilizes " rational " not only as he has defined it, but as the antonym of " superstitious "; and to say that a belief is superstitious implies that it should be rejected. If we anchor Hume's conclusions rigorously to the definition-scheme with which he began, his proof becomes trivial. Induction may not be rational in his sense, but is rational nevertheless in some sense equally important though hitherto unspecified. Conversely, however, if we define " rational " belief as belief provable by inductive argument, the vital point eludes us again; for although there is now no doubt that induction is rational, the doubt can still arise whether or not it should be adopted, and here Hume's arguments will have their original force, and neither less nor more.

Consider now two examples from moral philosophy. " Right " and " duty " are inter-defined by some formula such as " a man does his duty if he does that act which it is right for him to do ". In normal circumstances this is adequate, but doubt as to whether or not a man has done his duty might still arise in an anomalous case. It might arise if he does an act which is in itself wrong, but in this case is done from unusual motives. Normally it is done either from selfish motives, or through sheer carelessness; but in this instance the man has done it because after careful thought he believed that he really should. We may interpret " the act which was right for him to do " in one way and decide therefore that he has done his duty, or in the other way and decide that he has not. Whichever we do, however, our decision will lack its usual significance and force. Normally it is important and conclusive to say that duty has or has not been done; here, however, a listener may agree with whatever we say, and then add, " but after all . . . ". What he adds may in either case be as important as what we said ourselves, and its effect will be to render our own utterance nugatory. If we confer the term " duty " upon the man's conduct, such an important proviso has to be made that the grant is largely empty; if we refuse it, our refusal is nominal, for it leaves the important questions about his conduct entirely open.

Suppose, again, that one man injures another; the question is raised whether he should be blamed for the injury. Clearly he should be blamed if he was *responsible* for it; and one way in which he could be responsible is that he *deliberately* inflicted the injury. Then one may ask, Was his action deliberate? If it were difficult to decide this issue, one might enquire instead whether he *tried* to inflict the injury. Either of these might be regarded as depending on whether he had an *intention* to injure. If this part of his history were anomalous, if he had harboured malicious thoughts, indulged in spiteful day - dreams, treasured schemes of injuring, and known that this would tend to influence his future conduct, then, though this should itself be in the straightforward sense unpremeditated, one might be uncertain. There might be a tendency to say that he had an unconscious intention to injure. But this would not solve the original problem, for when it was posed the relations between responsibility and unconscious intentions had not been prescribed. Even if they were now to be prescribed the difficulty might not be over, for in the given case it might be impossible to decide whether the intention were unconscious or not ; and this not because we could not obtain the evidence we desired, but, having all the evidence we could imagine, we were at a loss how to describe it.

These examples illustrate well-known tendencies in philosophical discussion. A set of expressions is precisely defined, each expression by reference, at one step or at more, to the others ; and then sentences constructed from these expressions are manipulated as if in a formal calculus, and certain conclusions drawn. But the inter-definitions enshrine only a closed set of criteria selected from the open set which progressively describe the tendencies of usage for each word ; and in consequence the constructed language-model always leaves some linguistic forces out of account. Given an anomalous case, these suppressed tendencies (which may normally only reinforce the recognized criteria) become of considerable and perhaps predominant importance ; and it is usually possible to reveal them by selecting some link between a part of the crystallized vocabulary and other expressions outside it. In fact, we construct a rival model. In each of the above examples this double process can be traced : a particular anomalous case where the unacknowledged forces are powerful is taken, and so exploited as to show how strongly the enshrined usages conflict with others embedded firmly in ordinary language. Ingenuity can doubtless find, sooner or later, tendencies conflicting with every possible language-model. When one remembers that the conflict is between recognized and unrecognized criteria of usage, and that criteria of usage formulate habits of usage, and that habits are both acquired and eradicated by a perhaps lengthy process of conditioning, then one ceases to expect that any short method will give the victory to one side or the other. Victory can only be obtained by that process of further conditioning which is called persuasion. This is why some philosophical writings are full of expressions like " surely ", " an important sense ", " an unplausible view ", " common sense ", and " the plain man's moral consciousness "; or of persuasive examples, exhortations, objurgations, and rhetorical appeals; and it is what philosophers have in mind when they suggest that philosophical arguments consist in recommending linguistic usages. Each participant in the discussion develops his own model, and the easiest way to increase its attractiveness is to expose the weaknesses of its rivals — a process always guaranteed of some success.

It has been recognized, in several recent discussions of these problems, that an over-rigid systematization of language produces these shifts of meaning; and therefore that, at least between certain expressions and types of sentence, we must be satisfied with relations less sharp than those of logical entailment or incompatibility.[1] Any attempt, for example, to analyse material-object sentences exhaustively into sentences referring only to sense-data over-simplifies the subtlety and complexity of language. Similarly there are no precise logical relations between statements about dispositions and others about performances; or statements about feelings, and those about behaviour expressing those feelings; or between natural laws, and statements about particular positive or negative instances; or between statements about approval or disapproval, and others about right or wrong. A certain set of sense-datum sentences lends credence to a material-object sentence, or argues against it; or certain observations

---

[1] See especially F. Waismann, " The Many-level Structure of Language " in *Synthese* (Amsterdam), 1946, and " Verifiability " (more particularly pp. 119-134), *Proceedings of the Aristotelian Society*, Supp. Vol. 19 (1945).

lend credence to a scientific generalization. But because there is always the possibility of a surprise departure from the normal concomitances and regularities, arguing for or against can never reach the level of a relation in deductive logic. The various types of sentence constitute so many disparate linguistic *strata*, between which there is no rigorous interlocking. Within each stratum there may be precise logical relations; but in moving from one to another we pass through a region where outlines are necessarily blurred, if language is not to be simplified beyond point of usefulness.

These linguistic strata have already appeared in the present discussion, though mentioned in different terms. They are constituted from the alternative expressions which are equally applicable to the same situation.[1] Thus a certain situation may be described either by material-object expressions, or by sense-datum expressions. By " sense-datum expressions " will be meant here any such words as " patch " (when used of colour), " shadow ", " sparkle ", " glow ", " flicker ", and so on, that could be used to describe what one sees, without making reference to, and thereby asserting the existence of, any material objects. Again, a person's conduct over a period may be described by dispositional words, or by enumerating particular actions. As there is a tendency for these alternative expressions, if once jointly applicable, to be so regularly, they may be used as mutual criteria and the applicability of one argues for that of others; but since this tendency is never overwhelmingly strong, the relation can never be as strong as entailment.

It is possible, to some degree, to describe the features of ordinary language, discussed above, in terms of disparate linguistic strata; and to do so is illuminating. But unless certain qualifications are made, the strata may themselves be over-systematized, and reintroduce into language a rigidity

[1] See the abbreviated list on p. 140.

that they were deliberately invented to avoid. In the first place, several " alternative expressions " may belong to the same language-stratum; and because of this, sharp logical relations do not always obtain, even between expressions in one stratum. This happens in various ways. For example, I am uncertain whether or not I am seeing a cat. It would be possible for me to describe experiences of cat-like sense-data in an explicitly sense-datum language, and then say that these experiences lent credence to but did not conclusively establish the existence of the cat. This I should probably do if I feared the kind of deception connected with hallucinations. But if I feared another sort I might enumerate that I could see the legs, and the head, the tail, and the body, and so on; though I might still remain uncertain whether or not I saw a real and live cat. This time I use only material-object words, but I do not suppose that the sentences in which they occur entail that I see the cat. I should suppose only that they lent credence to this conclusion. This language would be appropriate if I expected to see not a hallucinatory cat, but a dead stuffed cat, or a waxwork cat, or a lynx. Using the sense-datum vocabulary revealed one sort of uncertainty; another could be revealed by using only the material-object stratum.

Conversely, " this is a chair " does not entail " this has legs, a seat, and a back ", but argues for it in a way similar to, though not identical with, that in which it argues for certain future experiences. " This is a chair " and " this is a bed " are not logically incompatible (chair-beds actually exist), but the two sentences tend to exclude each other. One sort of queer case tends to make these jointly applicable, and a different sort of queer case tends to make applicable all the usual sentences describing cat-like sensations, and also the sentence " but no cat is there ". Again, material-object words have similar implications, because objects have similar properties. For example, it is not generally possible for two material objects to occupy the same region in space; and therefore, although a material-object sentence which gave a location at X, and a sense-datum sentence giving the same location but mentioning apparently conflicting sense-qualities might only argue against each other, two sentences like " object A is at x " and " object B is at x " are as a rule strictly incompatible. But this does not hold good of sentences which refer to liquids and gases; sometimes not, of those which refer to solids. In certain circumstances books and book-worms, or books and bullets, may be in the same place; here the excluding formula only emphasizes that the exception is exceptional. Or suppose that a block of ice is placed on a block of warm chalk of the same shape, until the ice melts and is absorbed, and then the chalk is cooled until the water freezes. Any attempt here to keep rigidly to the usual implications of being a solid only transforms what is usually a help into a hindrance.

A similar absence of strictly logical relations can sometimes be traced between material-object sentences which mention colours. Imagine a shade of mauve just intermediate between red and blue. Everyone who, on being shown the colour, was told that it was a shade of red, accepted this statement; and everyone told it was a shade of blue, accepted this instead. It is well known that experiences can be modified or determined, within small limits, by what we are told to expect, or how it is described for us. Would not an object of this colour prove that sometimes " this object is red " and " this object is blue " are not strictly incompatible, but only tend to exclude each other; and that they may, in an unusual case, both be true? Perhaps this would also be shown by an object which persistently and systematically looked scarlet to some observers and ultramarine to others. One might object that the possibility that " this is red " and " this is blue " should be compatible depends on imaginary and fanciful instances; but this is almost equally true of the possibility that " this *is* red " and " this *looks* blue " should be compatible. Naturally the covert qualities of language become conspicuous only in unusual conditions.

Relations less sharp than those of deductive logic, but traceable within a single linguistic stratum, are not confined to sentences about material objects. The existence of a complex disposition, like " being hypochondriac ", or " being neurotic ", is not entailed by the proved existence of several or indeed an indefinite number of more specific dispositional tendencies. The relation is again one of arguing for (perhaps very strongly). There remains always, however, an element of doubt; rather as in enumerating the parts of a cat, but still wondering if the animal really is a cat; or in enumerating the parts of an animal that has been dissected, and still wondering whether perhaps it is a new species. Nor does one dispositional quality rigidly exclude even those which most seem its contraries: " being patient " and " being impatient " would, as we have seen, be only a first crude attempt, and subsequently be avoided; but " being patient " and " being irritable " are not strictly incompatible. They jointly constitute just that refinement of the first pair by virtue of which they do no more than argue against each other, and can therefore be reconciled in the unusual case. Similarly two sentences which describe feelings or emotions may be apparent contraries, but not mutually exclude each other. " I am glad " and " I am sad " are compatible, in the anomalous case of " mixed feelings ". Conversely " I am glad " does not entail " I am not sad ". Or again, " this is beautiful " and " this is ugly " are compatible for an object of " hideous beauty "; well known to poets of the nineteenth century, if less so to philosophers of the twentieth.

That the language-strata are not internally homogeneous may be seen in another way. Two words may belong to the same stratum, but sentences which are identical except that one contains the first word, and the other the second, may entail and exclude expressions of different types; and questions appropriate to the first word are not appropriate to the second. It was, indeed, this absence of homogeneity which led to the absence of sharp logical relations between material-object sentences.

For example, if a certain word belongs to the material-object stratum, it is sometimes permissible to ask questions about the edges or surfaces of an object denoted by it, but not always. This is permissible if the object is a solid or liquid, but not if it is a free gas (unless the gas is in the form of a flame), nor if it is a vapour, smoke, mist, or fog (unless this is quite unusually dense and well-defined). Under these circumstances the question becomes inapplicable. But since this is so, these material objects cannot be said to have either a precise shape or a precise size. Nor, for example, is it possible to count the number of the flames which come from a burning fire; though we can say that there are few or many, or that one fire has more than another, and the relation denoted here by "more than" has some of the properties of the mathematical relation "greater than". Nor is it possible to give the exact location or boundaries of those currents of warm air which appear as heat shimmers over the grass on a hot day. The distinction is sometimes made between the material-object and the sense-datum strata, that in the former precise details about shape, size, number, and location are always obtainable (at least after repeated investigation), while in the latter they are not. But in these respects "flame" and "mist" and "gas", though they are plainly material-object words, resemble sense-datum words.

Besides these there are similar variations within the sense-datum vocabulary. But they are easily obscured by considering not the whole vocabulary actually in use as sense-datum words, but a philosopher's vocabulary which is made artificially consistent, and in which the only words appear to be " patch " and " sense-datum " itself. First, expressions of this kind differ widely in their capacity to be linked with spatial references. Thus one may say that a " patch " of colour is in a certain place, almost as if it were a material object. An (unreal) " image " seen in a lens appears to be a quite determinate distance behind the lens. But the " flicker " seen before a rotated Maxwell colour-disc, just before this reaches a speed at which it turns white in appearance,[1] can be related to the spatial positions of material objects only in a very general way : one can say that the flicker appears in front of the disc, but not how far in front. An " after-image " seen with our eyes open after we have gazed at a bright light, cannot be described as either in front of, upon, or behind the object which it blots out ; its apparent distance is entirely indeterminate, and only its apparent direction can be specified. Last, *muscae volitantes* and other similar effects are indeterminate as regards both apparent distance and direction ; for they are never quite still, and the eye cannot focus upon them.

Again, it is not true that precise criteria of shape, size, or number are never applicable to descriptions in a sense-datum vocabulary. Sometimes they must be applicable, because applying them to material objects depends on our having precisely determinate sense-experiences. We can only say that two bars, for example, are of precisely the same length, because we observe that two visible marks are precisely coincident ; and an experience of this kind is as easily describable in a sense-datum terminology as the indeterminate experience of seeing stars. Therefore, like material-object descriptions, some sense-datum descriptions are determinate as regards these qualities and others are not. Nor is it true that sense-datum expressions, as ordi-

---

[1] I owe this illustration, though not its use here, to Dr. Waismann.

narily used, apply only to one person's private experience. It may be made a rule of usage that several persons can see the same object, while each must be said to see a different " sense-datum " ; but this is a philosophical refinement. Ordinary speech does not utilize it, and in ordinary speech several persons could perfectly well say that they saw the same shadow, or the same rainbow, or the same mirage. They would not thereby commit themselves to the view that a shadow, a rainbow, or a mirage were objects like mists or flames ; much less like waterspouts.

Last, though one may make it a rule of usage that " I am sensing a blue sense-datum " and " I am sensing a white sense-datum " are logically incompatible if both are determined alike as regards time and apparent location, this will be a rule for the single word " sense-datum " but will not bind the whole class of expressions of which it is considered typical. It is perfectly permissible, for example, to say that one sees a blue *patch* and a white *lustre* in the same place ; one would in fact say " I see a blue patch with a white lustre " ; and here the two sense-datum words are conjoined though differently qualified.

Similar considerations apply to disposition words and to the varied forms of generalization. There is not merely one form of disposition word, but several ; and between them relations of entailment and incompatibility do not exist. Thus although a schoolboy cannot have both a habit of working neatly and a habit of not working neatly, he may have a habit of working neatly, and a slight tendency to work carelessly. This means that his normal style is subject to intermittent breakdowns of a consistent and recognizable kind. Similarly there are several varieties of empirical generalization. A generalization like " people always run after new fashions " need not be adjusted if individual negative instances are found, or even if from time to time a fashion is invented which never attracts anyone. But " swallows fly to Africa in winter ", though unaffected by an isolated swallow who contravened it, would need adjustment or supplementation if even in one year all the swallows stayed, and none migrated. If even one negative instance is found to, for example, Kepler's Laws of planetary motion, a change or supplementary account must necessarily be provided or posited; but it would be possible to assume the influence of some unobserved causal agent, such as a " dark body ", of a kind whose activity is describable within the existing corpus of knowledge. This would not be true of a generalization which exhaustively specified every concomitant condition, and might be tested in an experiment where every known factor was controlled. Here a single negative result disproves the generalization, unless one posits some causal influence of a quite new kind. In every instance there appears to be a different logical relation between the general propositions, and those which describe the particular cases.

There is a third point of importance about language-strata, and this, indeed, might explain some though not all of the linguistic elasticities discussed above. Certain words belong ambiguously to more than one of the strata. The words " legs ", " body ", and " tail ", used in describing a possibly waxwork cat, illustrate this tendency. Here it is uncertain whether they describe appearances or denote material objects which may or may not be those required to constitute a cat that was both real and alive. It is uncertain, because no answer was given prior to the utterance, as the question had not been raised. Similarly the expression " heat-shimmer " may belong to the sense-datum or to the material-object stratum; for the question is open, whether it is more akin in its use and implications to " flame " which is fairly definitely a material-object word, or to, for example, " reflection " or " iridescence ", which fairly definitely is not. Words like " appearance " and " figure " are useful just because their status is explicitly ambiguous. Those who investigate supernatural phenomena use " appearance " to emphasize that they leave the question open, whether they are describing simply their own experiences, or some strange but quasi-material object. " Patch " and " surface " are used sometimes as unequivocally material-object words, occasionally as sense-datum words, usually without our determining which.

Three points have been stressed about language-strata. First, that between statements within a single stratum there are sometimes relations less rigid and sharp than entailment and incompatibility, and like those relations of arguing for or against which hold between statements in different strata ; second, that the vocabulary of a single stratum is not always homogeneous, and in consequence that questions appropriate to some members of the vocabulary are inappropriate for others, and the implications of sentences containing different members of the same linguistic stratum are sometimes different in kind ; third, that some expressions do not belong outright to one stratum, but are of intermediate status. All these features point to the same conclusion. Philosophers do not discover in ordinary language a hierarchy of linguistic strata completely formed, but an immense variety and a complete absence of system. They do not discover, but invent or construct the strata ; and they do this by prescribing exactly what shall and shall not be implied by various expressions, and by grouping large numbers of different expressions together, treating them alike, and prescribing similar powers for them. Were this to be done completely, the ambiguities and heterogeneity noticed above would disappear. But in fact the process of assimilation cannot ever be completed, even to the extent of producing a small number of perfectly distinct and homogeneous strata. It can be pushed so far, because our experience manifests a certain variable degree of regularity, and this is embedded in the unsystematized use of language. The relations between stones and books are sufficiently like those between stones and stones, for

" book " and " stone " to be classified as words of the same kind. There is a less powerful analogy between " stone " and " water ", but the differences between them are less far-reaching and pervasive than between, say, " stone " and " shadow ". Conversely, though " shadow " and " sheen " have slightly different powers, there is a fairly strong analogy between them.

It seems as if, in the initial and unsystematized condition of language, there were as many strata as there were different expressions. Systematization reduces this number by assimilating the status of one word to that of another. The classes of material-object words, sense-datum words, disposition words, approval words, ethical words, and the rest are built up : and parallel with them, various distinct types of sentence in which they are to be used. This process of regimentation may sometimes be advantageous, but can easily be the reverse ; some expressions there will always be that can only enter the scheme if their significance is slightly modified, and others (like " appearance " and " miscellaneous ") whose value is that they mitigate the rigidity of systems.

The remainder of this chapter is concerned with certain little-discussed portions of our language as a whole : precise notations, usually non-verbal, which do not contain the ambiguities and vaguenesses inherent in the verbal language. In these sub-languages, as they might be called, ostensive definitions can often be rigorous and complete. The inter-definitions of terms, and their consequent relations in the closed system, are exact and precise ; the system as a whole works like a logical calculus. But we can construct such a system only if we agree to restrict the range of its duties. We accept as a full description what normally would not count as full ; and thus we attempt to exclude the risk that better acquaintance with the objects we speak of will oblige us to describe them afresh. That risk, however, cannot be removed by a mere fiat ; in different cases it assumes more or less importance, and is met by one expedient or another.

These sub-languages include arithmetic and geometry, as far as they are used for descriptive purposes; chess notation; musical notation; the technical directions in a knitting pattern; morse notation; conventionalized maps, to some extent; and the notation used for describing games of cards. When arithmetic is used descriptively, certain restrictions are imposed. If groups of objects are counted, all differences between them except those revealed by the process of counting are deemed irrelevant. A class, about the number of whose members there is an uncertainty, is never accepted as a border-line case of the number of objects in question; if the uncertainty cannot be conclusively removed, the objects are classified as not countable, and the use of the precise sub-language is withdrawn. Thus we should not say that two groups of flames lent support to " $4 + 3 = 8$ ", if, when we counted the groups separately, one seemed to have four flames, the other three, but when the two groups were set close together there seemed to be eight. We should say " these flames cannot be exactly counted ". We refuse to apply the precise language whenever its use would jeopardize its precision. Alternatively, we posit the occurrence of physical events which exactly explain away the discrepancies. If we measure spatial figures, and obtain results which conflict with the theorems of our geometry, we simply explain the discrepancy away by speaking of " errors of measurement " (in other words, non-geometrical factors which the notation does not profess to describe); the formal relations are never weakened from entailments to probabilities. Finally, if very unusual observations in applying arithmetic or geometry persuade us to adopt a new mathematical system, this also will be precise. The facts do not disprove or weaken the old system, but cause us to find another.

Arithmetic and geometry are distinctive in their entire

absence of verbal comment ; they contain, even in their
descriptive uses, no asides.   In chess and music, asides
must be allowed, because events and characters which the
precise notation does not attempt to cover may temporarily
assume importance.   When this occurs, the notation is
supplemented.   In chess, the formula " j'adoube " is used
when a player adjusts the position of a piece without
moving it in the sense covered by the notation.   But since
it is not so covered, a perfectly complete and authentic
description of the game can properly omit mention of it ;
and conversely, chess-notation does not even profess to
describe what happens when a player adjusts the position
of a piece without playing it.   In musical notation, precise
and exhaustive descriptions of a melodic sequence are
possible from a certain artificially restricted viewpoint.   As
between notes played on a piano and written on paper, it
is always possible to say categorically whether the description is true or false ; different descriptions sharply exclude
each other, and a description in one clef entails another in
another clef.   But this precise language has to be supplemented by a vague and quasi-verbal language which refers
to the interpretation and *nuance* of a given performance ; and
these additions, simple or elaborate, cannot be exhaustive
and precise.   They are necessarily more or less generic ;
and there is not even any conventional device at all for
noting certain aspects of a performance, such as that a
player produced a hitherto unheard timbre.   To refer to
such an aspect as this, one would have to rely not on the
non-notational part of musical recording, but on the
ordinary verbal language ; and that this is a different kind
of description can be seen in that the recorder would not
know where on his page of music to write his comment,
whereas every normal comment has a conventional place.
By such additions, the features which cannot be assimilated
to a precise notation are indeed recorded, but the problems
typical of ordinary language return.   Sometimes, again, the

musical notation itself tends to lose its precision, because it is distinctively interpreted. A string player plays C sharp a little sharp, when he plays in a certain key; a wind player " humours " a certain note. This is a first step towards fusing the precise notation and the interpretative additions; and the notation acquires the looseness of ordinary language, to the degree to which it occurs.

Other precise notations sometimes require additions of a similar less precise kind. Thus in a knitting formula, which is itself of precise application, one occasionally finds such more generic directions (in brackets) as " cast off these stitches loosely ". With this phrase we return, at a step, to the endemic vagueness of the verbal language. Similar additions can be traced in a morse operator's description, by means of a series of letters, of what he hears through his headphones. Normally his concern is only to record a pattern of dots and dashes. Every other feature is irrelevant, and (except for a difficulty mentioned below) his experience is from this point of view precisely and exhaustively describable. Consequently his record is as precise as the record of a melody on a musical stave. But if he has some special concern, such as a desire to help another operator to identify the sending station, he will make additional and unprecise descriptive notes about peculiarities in the sending, such as its tone or speed, or the characteristic length of its dots and dashes. Again, in simplified map-making there are conventional signs and devices which are at least intended to have precise meanings and to constitute exhaustive disjunctions. On some maps, for example, every church is marked as having either a spire, or a tower, or neither. On military maps, the presence of a new division might be recorded simply by the addition of a flag. But in certain circumstances these conventional simplifications must be supplemented and qualified by descriptive notes ; and these reintroduce the uncertainties avoided by the conventional sign. The verbal language

used in heraldry also illustrates these features. Precise
and exhaustive descriptions are possible in this language,
because it claims to describe only certain features of
escutcheons, and because escutcheons themselves must
have sharply distinct colours and shapes. When an alleged
specimen does not lend itself to such description, it is not
described in other terms, but is refused the name of
escutcheon. Were two escutcheons to differ only in respects
not describable in the language, they would be grouped as
one. In this field, powerful legal and other forces make
for precise notation, if not by one means, then by another.

Recording card-games has some particularly interesting
features. A written record of a game of bridge, for example,
is a precise description of some features of the whole
performance, but makes no mention of other features.
That a bridge-player made his bid in a peculiar tone of
voice, or laid down a card in an unusual way, is ignored.
The record of the game consists of a table with four columns
and thirteen rows. The columns are conventionally
marked to denote the respective players, the succession of
rows indicates the sequence of tricks, and conventional
signs within the table record what cards were played. A
whole table is the authentic record of a game ; no supplementation is possible. But in this case the limitation
comes from a rule of play. Every feature which cannot
be recorded in this notation is deemed improper. However
hesitatingly or confidently a player makes a bid or plays a
card, the effect and significance of his conduct is unchanged.
In practice, of course, a player might be able to convey
information to his partner by these means, but he is
forbidden to do so. Everything which is a proper part of
the game (even, for example, giving information to one's
partner by playing an agreed convention) is recorded in the
notation of the game ; everything which cannot be so
recorded is prohibited. If anything occurs which influences
the course of the game, but is not describable in the nota-

tion, we insist that the whole performance is not bridge at all, but, at best, some new game. If the facts become unamenable, that is, they are rejected ; and fresh, amenable facts called for, so that the recognized game can go on.

This can happen in other ways. If a game were played with very worn and tattered cards, it might be impossible to say whether, for example, the six of hearts or of diamonds had been played. But although such cards could doubtless be used in some form of amusement, they are useless for ordinary card-games. There might be a set of chessmen so big that they could not be placed unambiguously on a chess-board ; but if so, no attempt would be made to play chess with them. A chess player might attempt to win greater freedom of action for himself by placing his pieces ambiguously on the board ; but his opponent would refuse to continue the game. A musical instrument might play out of tune in so haphazard a manner that it was impossible to describe a performance upon it by writing notes on an ordinary musical stave. But if this were so, we should say that the instrument could not produce music at all. If the sender's morse exhibited occasional flaws, the receiving operator might guess, or leave blanks. But if the sending were worse still, it would not be classified as morse, and a new sending operator would be installed.

Thus an artificially constructed precise notation is always threatened, in one way or another, by the occurrence of events which it cannot fully describe. There is sometimes a strong practical incentive to employ it : we desire to use mathematical calculations, or we are interested only in certain features of our subject-matter, or we wish to play a conventional game. Then the precision and completeness of the notation are somehow preserved, and its patterns are not blurred by modifying it to fit the facts more closely. Sometimes (as in elections, when votes are counted without regard to the influence or acumen of the voters) this is achieved by an admitted simplification in classifying; sometimes (as when geometry is used in surveying) by positing just those unobserved events, referred to as " errors of measurement ", which preserve the original exactitude. Sometimes the precise notation may be supplemented by looser descriptive additions ; if so, its precision is partly safeguarded, but the primary description and the additions tend to merge. Sometimes we simply refuse to apply the notation when it cannot adequately describe all the relevant facts or events ; and, as in card or chess games, we produce suitably simple conditions artificially, by special equipment. If this equipment is misused so that its purpose is defeated, we insist on " playing again " ; that is, on further behaviour which the game-notation can exactly describe. If the equipment is defective or damaged, we replace it. In one way or another, if there is good reason for a precise notation, we find means to preserve it intact.

It is time to draw together the argument of this chapter. The origin of a systematized language is the desire to employ deductive methods in speaking of matters of fact. We may attempt the systematization in different ways; of which three, ostensive definition, verbal inter-definition, and restricted but precise notations, have been examined in detail. Of these, ostensive definition fails because the meaning of a word can never be determined with complete precision by producing samples. The samples cannot anticipate all the variations that the future may bring ; and renewed, more subtle attention, even to the finite set of given samples, may always reveal hitherto unnoticed analogies and differences between one set of samples and another.

The attempt to turn language into a quasi-calculus by mutual verbal definitions of its terms proved also not to be a complete success, though for other reasons. The initial effect is to produce what might perhaps be termed " vocabularies ", or finite sets of words, each member of which is related precisely to each of its fellows by unequivocal verbal formulae. But this precision is obtained at the price of a rigidity which means that new or anomalous configurations may not accord easily with the simplified model. When this occurs a word will, on the strength of the defining formula, be used although it cannot in this case have much of its normal force ; or withheld, although many of the normal reasons for using it exist. The use of the simplified model has created linguistic strains, which can be displayed by drawing attention to further expressions, equivalences, or turns of phrase, unrecognized in the model, but important in common speech. These illustrate tendencies of usage that have been ignored or suppressed ; but they revenge themselves, surreptitiously, by bringing about subtle shifts of meaning precisely sufficient to render nugatory the apparent precision of our diction, and the resulting conclusiveness of our deductions.

Nor can any such precise " vocabulary " be made self-contained. One may always draw, from the indefinitely varied resources of common speech, a fresh expression which links some of its members with words outside the system ; or a new configuration of fact or language may reveal the artificiality and stiltedness of what seemed beyond challenge. A precise sub-language is possible only when it is non-verbal (or at least has no element in common with ordinary language) ; and where also the described facts are made appropriate for such description, and are discarded if they cease to be so.

Any attempt whatever to systematize language exhaustively is doomed to failure ; and any attempt to systematize one part of it, so as to utilize deductive methods within a restricted field, is pushed forward against increasing strain and difficulty, and must be of limited scope. Moreover, even this partial systematization may have to be modified or discarded, if the event proves it excessive or misdirected. In all these respects, the analogy between using language and behaving in any other manner still persists. The claim that using symbols is only one form, though specialized, of behaviour in general, is confirmed by an internal study of the character of the verbal language. The systematization of language is exactly parallel to the ritualization of behaviour. If we confined our behaviour to ritual-actions, we should necessarily find either that it lacked subtlety, became inappropriate and meaningless almost without our knowing, was stilted, arbitrary, and puppet-like ; or that we could not act at all, except on certain artificially favourable occasions. There could no more be a perfectly precise and systematized language than a repertoire of rituals comprehensive enough to handle every human situation. It might be possible to complete the systematization of language, if its use were a unique activity. But it is impossible ; and this constitutes one further argument that using language is a part of behaviour in general, and has the character appropriate to its origin.

INDEX

A priori propositions, x, 166
Abstract general ideas, 2 f.
Acting, 100, 127
" All ", 146, 159, 160
" And ", 145
Austin, J. L., v, 34, 125
" Automatic " behaviour, 48, 53-4,
    58, 89, 110
  adapted intelligently, 110-12
Automatic sequences in thought,
    23-6, 35-7
Aveling, F., 38 f.

Belgion, M., 32
Berkeley, 1 f., 14, 16
Burt, C., 83, 84

Card-games, notation for, 185-6
Causal enquiries, 68 f.
Chess, 72, 183
Classifications, 161-2
Colour-words, 155-7, 161, 164-5,
    172, 174, 178
Communication, 107 f.
Comparisons, 18 f.
Concepts, xii, 16 f., 55
Conditions, standing, 69, 72, 80
  sufficient and necessary, 70 f.
Conjunctions, 144 f.
Cook-Wilson, 17
Counting, 125, 176, 182
Crawford, J. F., 33
Criteria, of intelligence, 96-106
  of meaning, 141 f.
Critical insight, 92
  testing of thought-sequences, 7 f.,
    26 f., 36
Croce, 55

Deduction in ordinary language,
    151-2, 155 f.
Definitions, 130-31, 155 f., 163-4
Describing, xiii, 124, 132 f.
Desires, 49-50
Dictionaries, 123, 131, 140
Dispositions, 72, 97 f.
" Disposition-words ", 149-50, 171,
    175, 178

" Distinction of reason ", 9 f.
Drill, military, 48, 93-4, 125

" Egocentric particulars ", 116-21
Entailment in ordinary language,
    171 f.

Facial expressions, 108 f.
Falsehood, 56, 158. *See* Truth
Fowler, H. W., 131
Fox, C., 31

Gesture, 108 f., 117 f.

Habit, 49-54, 59, 64, 87 f., 109 f.,
    151, 159
  senses of, 87 f.
Hampshire, S., 11
Hardie, W. F. R., 166
Heraldry, language used in, 185
Hevesi, J. L., v
Hobhouse, 65
Hume, 6 f., 14, 16, 168

Idea-series, 7 f.
  standard members of, 11 f.
" If ", 145
Imageless thought, 38, 41
Images, 2 f.
  " tactile ", 10
Imitation, 50-51, 53, 109
Implementation, 78 f.
Induction, 168
Insight, 65, 98 f.
Instantiation, 17-20, 34
Intelligence, causes of, 72 f.
  criteria of, 96-106
  in animals, 62 f.
  in behaviour, 72 f., 76-8, 87 f.,
    110-12
  in implementing plans, 78 f.
  in thinking, 74 f., 89, 94, 98-106
  lapsing into automatic behaviour,
    64, 114
  senses of, 88, 96
  -tests, 83
  -words, 81-3, 85
Introspection, 38, 54, 98 f.
Irony, 128